NEW HOLLAND
PROFESSIONAL floristry

floristry

Jacqueline Goss and Jane Wighton

NEW
HOLLAND

First published in 2008 by New Holland Publishers (UK) Ltd
London • Cape Town • Sydney • Auckland
www.newhollandpublishers.com

Garfield House
86-88 Edgware Road
London W2 2EA
United Kingdom

80 McKenzie Street
Cape Town 8001
South Africa

Unit 1
66 Gibbes Street
Chatswood
NSW 2067
Australia

218 Lake Road
Northcote
Auckland
New Zealand

ISBN 978 1 84537 878 3

Senior Editor **Sarah Goulding**
Designer **Lisa Tai**
Photographer **Shona Wood**
Production **Marion Storz**
Publishing Director **Rosemary Wilkinson**

10 9 8 7 6 5 4 3 2 1

Reproduction by Pica Digital Pte Ltd, Singapore
Printed and bound by Craft Print International Ltd, Singapore

contents

the philosophy

Many people dream of having a career in a creative and exciting industry, where one day's work is never the same as another. Floristry certainly provides that, and the thrill of unpacking boxes of gorgeous blooms is one of which we never tire. It's fantastic to be able to fulfil a bride's dream of her perfect wedding bouquet, or to be able to express in flowers the last gesture of affection for a deceased loved one. However, there are also the early mornings at the wholesale market and the late evenings with deadlines to meet, being wet and cold most of the day, and having hands which look twenty years older than your face! You also need to be fit and strong enough to be able to carry heavy vases of water and spend most of the day on your feet, but the passion for floral design will make up for all of this when you can look at a living piece of art and say, "I made that!".

Floristry is a job for everyone, whatever your age or sex. It is something that you can develop over a lifetime, a highly skilled profession with a sometimes modest salary but huge job satisfaction. There are many different courses now available at a number of institutions that can teach you floristry skills to whatever level you wish to achieve, whether you want to earn a living from it or just enjoy it as a hobby. You will always be learning, though – even once qualified, you must keep up with ever-changing designs and fashions, explore new, innovative products and be inspired by other designers. You must offer state-of-the-art designs alongside traditional techniques and materials, and retain the ability to adapt to each customer's individual needs. You must always be evolving, ready to learn new skills whilst mastering the basics.

It is difficult ensuring 100 per cent satisfaction for every customer, but striving for that is paramount to every successful business. Customers can be difficult, staff can be lethargic, business can be quiet or manic by turns. The floristry calendar allows us to be prepared for the obvious, such as St Valentine's Day, but a good florist will be busy all year round and customer satisfaction will be the catalyst for any business. Preparation and a good team are the keys to success, along with the experience that comes with time. Learn from your mistakes – always allow extra time and materials for mishaps and be prepared to make last-minute adjustments where necessary. Pulling off a big order can be a daunting task, but the buzz you get from doing it, the pride you will take in your work and the good feedback that you get always make it more than worthwhile.

We don't pretend to know it all, but in this book we share some ideas that we like and know to be successful. We hope that this collection of design ideas, technical advice and professional know-how will be of practical help, and inspire you to achieve your own goals in the world of floral design.

Jacqueline & Jane

“ It's fantastic to be able to fulfil a bride's dream of her perfect wedding bouquet... ”

01 general techniques

buying and choosing flowers

Whether you are buying stock from a wholesale market, retail shop or stall, there are some key points to consider which will ensure you get value for money and optimum usage from the materials you purchase.

1 Quality and condition

Don't be afraid to examine stock carefully to determine its freshness by lifting a stem or bunch from the container and checking for clean stems with no slime build-up or bad odour. If this is present but the flower heads are still good, you may want to negotiate a lower price – particularly if you are buying for practice purposes. Good quality material is undamaged, blemish-free and will have healthy-looking leaves and stems.

2 Buds or blooms?

How advanced you want your stock to be will be determined by what you are making. For instance, funeral tributes will need to be constructed using mainly open flowers, as they are needed for a short period of visual impact; gift bouquets, however, will contain a mixture of buds, intermediate and full blooms so that the recipient has both initial colour and some to come. Always be a little wary of buying very tightly-budded material – it may have been cut at nursery too early and may never open, so buds showing a little colour are always best.

3 Environmental conditions

It is a good idea to visit several shops or stands, comparing price, availability and varieties of material until you find one that best suits the work you do and your particular taste and style. Look at how they treat and present their stock, making sure that conditions are clean and well managed to ensure you are not buying diseased or damaged material. Anything you buy should be well wrapped for safe transportation.

4 Customer care

By establishing a good relationship with your regular supplier, they will be more likely to give you valuable advice on current trends and prices, stock variations and innovations that will ensure you are getting the best deal. They may even reserve stock at busy periods if they consider you to be a loyal customer, so it is in your interest to build a good rapport.

△ *Examine your materials carefully to make sure that they are fresh.*

5 Seasonal or special?

Although most varieties of stock can be obtained all year round (albeit at a premium if imported from abroad), for good quality and value for money it is advisable to choose materials which are in season. This also helps you as a florist to continually ring the changes in your designs, rather than always be using similar combinations. Of course there are staple components like roses, chrysanthemums and carnations which are invaluable as reliable sources of colour and structure, but when supplemented in spring with narcissi and sprigs of pussy willow, the design suddenly takes on a much fresher and more seasonal flavour.

There will be occasions, usually for wedding or venue commissions, when particular flowers are required which can only be force-grown at other times of the year than their normal seasonal flowering. These will always come at a much higher price, and this should be reflected in your charges.

care and conditioning

It is essential that all materials be conditioned appropriately to ensure that optimum appearance and lifespan are achieved for all your designs. The following steps should be taken as soon as possible after purchase.

★ Remove all packaging, including cellophane sleeves and tie bands, to allow material to breathe and to avoid bruising or crushing of stems and blooms.

★ Ensure that containers are clean, with sufficient fresh, tepid water containing flower food to provide minerals and guard against bacteria.

★ Any foliage which will be below the waterline should be removed, as well as all thorns and suckers or shoots along the stems, as these will draw off water before it reaches the flower heads.

★ Stems should be cut using a knife or floristry scissors at a slanted angle, to open up a large surface area for water to be taken up the stem. Material must then be put straight into water, or it will begin to seal up and prohibit this process.

★ Woody-stemmed foliage can be cut similarly with secateurs or chopped with an axe.

★ In warmer weather, blooms should be sprayed with a fine mist of water to enable additional moisture to be absorbed through the leaves and petals.

★ Flowers and plant materials should be allowed to stand in a bucket of water for a long drink before being arranged. Do not squash them tightly into a small bucket, though.

STORAGE AND AFTER-CARE

All fresh material should be kept in cool, shady conditions and out of direct sunlight, particularly if it is shining in through glass, which can scorch and wither leaves. It is not advisable to use a domestic refrigerator for storing flowers as they are too cold and will over-chill materials, causing them to perish. Specially-designed cold stores for florists are at a suitable temperature to enable stock to last longer than in normal conditions.

Wired wedding items should be well packaged in a box lined with paper and tissue which has been thoroughly misted with water and kept in a cool place, such as a garage or outhouse, until the bridal party is ready to leave. All designs arranged in foam should be kept topped up with water, periodically misted and any dead flower heads removed to encourage remaining buds to open and the life of the design to be prolonged.

Cut flowers and hand-tied bouquets in vases must have a water change every other day, with additional flower food added and stems re-cut before replacing in the container. In very warm weather, this may need to be done every day.

△ Cut stems at a slanted angle to increase water uptake.

the florist's toolkit

The tools of the florist's trade are many and varied, with new, innovative products appearing on the market all the time. However, a small, portable toolbox containing a few essential pieces of kit is perfectly adequate most of the time. Of course this will need to be supplemented by the addition of more specialized equipment appropriate to the job at hand, but it's amazing how technically inventive more experienced florists can be with their basic set of tools!

Initially, a good set of cutting tools are the first priority and these must include a penknife and a pair of industry-standard scissors which can deal with wires as well as woody stems. The addition of a good pair of secateurs for dealing with thicker foliage, as well as small dressmaking scissors which can be reserved for trimming ribbon neatly, would also be very useful. Next on the list must be a selection of wire bundles in several gauges and lengths for internal and external flower support, particularly for constructing all bridal designs from buttonholes to wedding bouquets. The most useful stub wires tend to be 71mm and 90mm gauge, and silver rose wires in a standard 36mm thickness. Having both stub and silver wire in a continuous length on a reel is essential for construction purposes.

With cutting and wiring tools collected, there must be a selection of fixing materials with which to secure and stabilize a variety of mediums into containers. The foremost of these must be 'pot tape', a strong, waterproof tape on a roll which is invaluable for holding foam in any type of container and a host of other situations, including the securing of hand-tied bouquets. Where tape is going to be too obtrusive, a sticky fixing medium is available on a reel which can be used in strips or moulded into the required shape to secure metal or plastic pin holders into the base of a dish or basket. Floral adhesives are available in a range of forms including cold glue in tubes, and those designed to be applied with a heated glue gun. With the increasing popularity of European design influences and their use of accessories, these glues are becoming an essential kit component of the modern and creative floral designer.

USEFUL TOOLS AND EQUIPMENT
① **Hot glue gun**
② **Floral foam for fresh flowers**
③ **Oasis Fix – florists' gum**
④ **Candles**
⑤ **Ribbons, poly-paper, satin and gutta-percha (a rubber-based tape for stem and wire binding)**
⑥ **Raffia**
⑦ **Rose strippers**
⑧ **Green twine**
⑨ **Posy holder**
⑩ **Water vial**
⑪ **Stub wires (left) and decorative wires (right)**
⑫ **Sticky tape and double-sided tape**
⑬ **Frogs (see page 64)**
⑭ **Tapes – waterproof pot tape and Stem-tex (a paper-based binding tape)**
⑮ **Pin holder**
⑯ **Scissors**
⑰ **Hair comb**
⑱ **Decorative pins**
⑲ **Silver reel wire**
⑳ **Florists' knife**

There is a large range of tapes on the market specifically for wired work, which will enable a florist to produce a smooth, neat finish and, at the same time, cover their construction techniques. These can be either paper-based or rubber and, when applied to wired stems, will also help to seal in moisture, thus enabling the work to be prepared in advance. In the case of bridal bouquets, for example, which are time-consuming to construct, this can make all the difference. In fact, it is entirely feasible for wired designs, if they are well packaged and kept cool until the ceremony, to last perfectly throughout the day – unlike tied items which can quickly wilt on a hot day with constant handling.

Added to these basic components, a host of other items will find their way into a florist's toolbox as a result of undertaking the vast range of commissions which present themselves. These may include pearl-headed pins, reels of decorative wires, various gift and care cards, orchid tubes and glass test-tubes, and perhaps the odd new gadget or gizmo to try. However, it must never be forgotten that the primary components are the flowers and foliage themselves, and whatever equipment and mechanics we use they must, above all else, serve us and not rule us in the accomplishment of our designs.

Containers

In the floristry industry there is a vast number of sundry items on the market including containers in all sizes, shapes and materials, from the most basic of plastic dishes custom-made to hold a block of foam, to expensive glassware and hand-thrown Italian pottery. With so much available, it is very easy to find a complementary container to suit any style of design. For example, a country-themed, cottage garden arrangement would look beautiful in a rustic basket, while a contemporary, minimalist tank vase could contain just a layer of roses.

Pictured is just a small representation of the types of container available at any florist wholesaler.

▷ *A small selection of the many containers available.*

general techniques **15**

health and safety

It is required by law that adequate training is provided by employers, and it is essential that you are aware of any risks to yourself, colleagues and customers. You will find that most health and safety issues are common sense and instinctive.

Please consider the following when making any arrangements.

★ That you have selected the correct tool and equipment for use.

★ That the tools and equipment are clean and sharp and have been well maintained, ready for use.

★ Any lifting should be carefully addressed; e.g. you may need help setting up or removing items from a venue.

★ You must be dressed appropriately for the job. Wear an apron to protect your clothes and gloves to protect your hands.

★ When working on site at a venue, carry a condensed size toolbox carrying essential items only, and a miniature first aid box for small accidents.

★ Work at the correct height for your body. Do not stretch up or down unnecessarily – this will cause strains and you may knock something over.

△ Keep your tools sharp at all times.

△ Always advise your customers of the dangers of lighting candles.

★ Keep a cork or sleeve over your knife blade and always keep your scissors closed when not in use.

★ Take care when using candles in arrangements. Do advise your customers of the dangers of leaving flames unattended, and where possible avoid lighting the arrangements until the last minute, ensuring that it is placed in a clear, open area.

★ Wash your hands after touching all plant and flower materials and be aware of touching your face before washing your hands.

★ When using spray cans such as leaf shines or decorative colour sprays, use them in a well-ventilated area or outside if possible.

★ Tell people where you are working if you are working on an assignment alone, and when to expect you back.

design elements and principles

There are three main factors involved in making a successful floristry feature: the design itself (the shape, style, colour, etc.); the setting; and the theme. All of these factors must be considered for any design, as well as taking time to speak to the customer to incorporate any personal wishes. Our best advice would be to make visits to the venue and have various consultations with the customer to ensure that what you are planning is suitable, desirable and achievable. This will also give you the opportunity of discussing themes and budgets.

Design determines the way we choose and use our materials to the best advantage, achieving maximum visual appeal. Every design a florist makes is subject to a budget, however, and this is something that is unique to each customer. Whatever the budget, good design will enable you to make something truly individual and tailored to your customer's needs.

The elements of design should be used as a guide to creating beautiful pieces. Once they have been mastered, the florist can use them in any way to create his or her own particular style. These elements are:

★ **Colour**
★ **Form**
★ **Space**
★ **Texture**

The principles of design are the technicalities behind designs, and are essential to any piece and the overall outcome. These principles are:

★ **Balance**
★ **Proportion**
★ **Rhythm**
★ **Contrast**
★ **Dominance**
★ **Harmony**

A good arrangement should have elements of all these things, so it is important to perfect your flower arranging theory whilst also working on your techniques. The following pages look at each of the main elements and principles of design in turn.

△ *Learning about the elements and principles of design will help to ensure that you create original, eye-catching arrangements.*

Colour

We relate to colour in our everyday lives both consciously and subconsciously. Think for a moment about the colours that you don't like. Why do you not like those colours? There are colours that we like on other people but would never wear ourselves, while a sofa that looks great in a shop window doesn't always suit our home. Fashion designers will agonize over the correct shade as they strive to achieve their 'look', as will interior designers for the right look in each room. Perhaps we associate a colour with a memory of something unpleasant? Colours can be connected to smells and trigger adrenaline inside us, and they can also stimulate the brain. Colours are strongly linked to our emotions, which is why colour theory is often used in therapy.

Now think about the colours that you do like. How do you feel when you think of the colours you are drawn to? Most people associate pale pink with babies; do you? If you were in a white room, how would you feel? Would you feel comfortable? Would the white be soothing, calm and fresh? Or would you find it over-stimulating, frightening, hostile and clinical? There is a similar divergence with the colour red. How does red make you feel? Some would argue that red is associated with passion and love, whereas others see it as anger and danger.

As a florist, colour is one of the main ingredients of a design, and if you do not get it right the outcome can be a disaster. The impact that colour makes will be the first thing that your customer remembers. Always bear in mind that what you may like in colours, your customer may not. It is important to give the customer as much information as possible so that they are completely in agreement with your plans. They should feel part of the design process and enjoy working with you towards a common goal. A good tip is to show them swatches of cloth against vases and flowers so that they can understand exactly your intentions. There is nothing worse than an dissatisfied customer, which can lead to bad publicity. If you have planned the colour schemes well, and taken into account all the other elements and principles of design, the impact of your professionalism will speak volumes and invite more work.

The more you think about colours, the more you will be able to use them effectively, and you will instinctively know which colours will suit and which will not. There are traditional designs that dictate certain colour schemes such

△ Colour, form and space all work well together in this long and low arrangement.

as the softer colours – pastel or autumnal, perhaps. Other more modern designs require a completely different look, such as stark, bold, vibrant and sometimes clashing and contrasting colours.

As colour is so important to your designs, it is essential that you consider this topic in more detail and explore combinations until you have a better understanding. See pages 22–25 for more on this subject.

Form

Form refers to the shape and structure of a design. Is it three-dimensional and able to be viewed all the way around, or is it more front-facing and viewed from the front only? For all-round designs such as a posy bowl (see pages 47–53) it would be best to use round-shaped flowers. This will achieve a 'round' look and feel to the design. Circular flowers such as roses, sunflowers, carnations, peonies and gerberas are often used in hand-tied bouquets, whereas for a front-facing triangle you will need tall, pointy flowers to achieve the right form. Flowers such as iris, veronica, gladioli, liatris, larkspur and monkshood would all be suitable for this design.

Above all, the materials used should be appropriate to the design and the desired outcome. You should consider your materials very carefully when purchasing them for their own individual structure and how they will behave with other materials. Remember that as the flower matures, the shape and form of the flower may also change, and that this will alter the outcome of the arrangement. As you become more experienced you will automatically select the right materials, but do not be afraid to break the mould and try a variety of flowers and foliage to achieve different outcomes.

Space

Space is the area that surrounds your design. A very small arrangement will look out of place and insignificant on a church altar, just as a very large bouquet would be unsuitable for a very small bridesmaid. The size of the arrangement is important to the placement in the venue. This is why it is essential to visit the venue to see for yourself whether the sizes are correct, and if the style and colour are suitable. You will then be able to make the correct decisions and advise your customer accordingly. They are relying on your judgement and skills to make their occasion the very best. Visiting the venue will also give you a chance to consider different containers for a particular look, allow

△ *Know your venue: a topiary tree such as this is perfect for a winter wedding, but less suitable for a small, intimate dinner party.*

you to assess the health and safety implications of assembling on site if applicable, and establish what access there is for delivery.

Space also refers to the area inside your arrangement and the materials as they lie against each other. Traditional designs have equal distance between materials, making them look quite static. This also looks blended and mixed, however, and easy on the eye. Modern work shows a variety of massing and tightly-packed flowers and also enormous spaces and areas between materials. This blocking of plants and flowers provides another interesting take on presentation and can make more of an impact by using well-defined colours and textures.

Texture

Texture relates to the substance of your design and enhances the visual impact. Texture can be either visual or actual. For actual texture we can touch something, and it feels as we expect it to. Visual texture is where you cannot touch the material but you can 'feel' the texture through memory. Your brain has 'touched' that material or something similar and reminds you that is soft, silky, spiky, rough, smooth or waxy, etc.

Texture is as important as colour when choosing materials and making up designs. You may wish to chose all the same textures and colours, often seen in contemporary work, and your placement of texture as with colour will determine whether it is viewed as a modern design or not. When placing similar textures together you create a dense effect, seen for

△ *This pedastal arrangement is visually very well balanced.*

instance with covering a foam base in funeral work, or a hand of roses for a bride to create a soft, smooth effect on the eye and a delicate touch to match the dress.

It would be wise to look in detail at the plant and flower material around you and consider each part in terms of shape, size, colour and texture. When choosing materials for your design you will have to consider all these factors equally – neglecting any one of them will alter the final outcome.

Balance

There are two kinds of balance: actual balance and visual balance. Actual balance is ensuring that your design is stable and will not topple over. Placing the correct size materials into your design and having the correct container to start with can ensure this. It is tempting to place all of your materials at the front of your design, but if you do not continue this through to the back, there is a danger that it will become too front-heavy and will pull forward.

Visual balance is achieved by placing materials equally around and through your designs. It may be that you choose to group your materials, and therefore the colour, size and

texture of the remaining area should match or balance it so that the eye is not overly drawn to one or the other areas. As with many aspects of floristry, this sense of visual balance is something that you will develop with time and experience.

Proportion

This means that the size of your design should be appropriate to both container and place setting. The scale of the materials used should also be considered to ensure that the sizes of materials are equal, or used *en masse* to balance an area of dominance.

Rhythm

Rhythm within a flower arrangement is the movement created by the positioning of the materials arranged together. This can be achieved by distorting the shape of leaves by folding, plaiting, rolling or looping, thereby creating movement as the eye roves over the distance between materials and follows the line and shape of each material.

Contrast

This is the difference between materials when placed next to each other. It may be the colour, the size, the texture, or even the shape; perhaps all. It is actually the stimulus that makes a design interesting. Too much contrast can make the design no longer balance, however, so this must be achieved carefully.

Dominance

Dominance is the main focus of attention within the arrangement. It could be colour, for example, or size. This is why we refer to our main flower as the focal point or the dominant feature. All the other components of the arrangement should be secondary.

Harmony

Harmony is the unity of your materials and the overall appearance of the finished design. The design should be pleasing to the eye, and all of the preceeding factors should have been accounted for during assembly. Harmony is also achieved by using the right materials for the occasion, and making sure that the design is sympathetic to its display area. Again, another reason to visit the venue or have detailed conversations with your customer.

◁ *Getting the proportion right is crucial to an arrangement's success.*

colour theory

Colour is such an integral part of floristry that it's important to understand a little more about how it works. Your designs will succeed or fail depending in a large part on whether you get this right or wrong, so pay attention!

Primary colours

The most important colours are the primary colours, from which all the others derive: red, blue and yellow. They are pure – that is, no other colours mixed together can reproduce them. They are also equidistant on the colour wheel. The other nine colours are composed of mixtures of these three.

Secondary colours

Secondary colours are made by mixing two primary colours together in equal parts. They are orange (red and yellow), purple (blue and red), and green (blue and yellow).

Tertiary colours

There are six tertiary colours which can be made by mixing one primary colour with one secondary colour, in equal parts.

These create red-orange, yellow-orange, yellow-green, blue-green, blue-violet and red-violet.

Neutral colours

Black, white and grey are neutral colours, used to add light or remove light from a colour. Tints can be created by adding white to any colour; tones can be created by adding grey to any colour; and shades can be created by adding black to any colour. Using these colours in our colour schemes enables us to enhance our designs and shapes by creating the effect of receding or advancing colours. For example, by adding white the design becomes illuminated, and lighter colours will advance towards the eye. Alternatively, darker colours will disappear and create a feeling of distance in the arrangements.

△ *Monochromatic colours*

colour combinations

To establish effective arrangements and display colours to their full advantage, you should familiarize yourself with the various possible combinations. Use a colour wheel to help you, and make a list of flowers and their colour variations.

By using different combinations of colour, you can create any number of different effects. Listed here are some of them.

Monochromatic – This is established by using tints, tones and shades of all one colour or hue.

Analogous – This is three or four sections on the colour wheel that are adjacent to one another, therefore creating a group of colours that have one pure hue plus an additional secondary and tertiary colour.
E.g. Red/white/pink/ruby/dusty pink

Complementary – These colours lie opposite each other on the colour wheel and have equal distance between them.
E.g. Yellow/violet

Polychromatic – This is an effective combination using as many of the colours as possible.
E.g. Red/blue/green/yellow/violet/turquoise/terracotta/plum/lime/crimson

Split complementary – This is achieved by using a colour and two others that lie either side of its natural opposite colour.
E.g. Red/turquoise/lime

Triadic – This is created by using three colours at equal distance on the colour wheel.
E.g. Red/yellow/blue

Tetradic – This is established by using four colours that are separated by equal distance on the colour wheel. This is also

△ Analogous colours

△ Complementary colours

known as double complementary.
E.g. Yellow/terracotta/violet/turquoise

Near complementary – This is created by using one colour and adding one of the two colours beside its complementary colour.
E.g. Red/turquoise

Black, white and grey are referred to as neutral colours. These are not colours as such, but used to darken or lighten arrangements. These also help to add depth to an arrangement by incorporating tints, tones and shades to advance or recede the other colours. Too much white can be overwhelming and overpower other colours in a design, but used carefully it can help liven up an arrangement by adding luminosity to what would otherwise have been regarded as a dark design. Alternatively, too much dark can make flowers disappear and the arrangements seem dull and unattractive, unless it is balanced carefully with other shades.

△ *Split complementary colours*

△ *Analogous colours*

lighting and colour alteration

Not only do we florists want to express a message through our flowers, but we also want to create a mood. Colour affects our senses greatly, and the combination of colours you use will alter the environment in which the flowers are placed. This is where floristry becomes part of interior design, and planning the correct arrangement for the right setting is a crucial part of our work.

Light is absorbed by the eye and sends messages to the brain, stimulating the nervous system and causing various reactions. For example, bright lights make us concentrate more and be attentive, whereas dim lights are more likely to make us drowsy and slow. Light therefore makes us react physically, and colour emotionally. Light changes all day depending on the time of day and the season. When the light levels fade, we rely on the electrical form, and this will also affect the ambience and the colour of the flower materials, changing the overall impression of your work. It is vital that you remember this when making designs for a party.

Artificial lighting

There are four main types of artificial lighting, all of which will affect your designs in different ways. They are as follows.

GENERAL LIGHTING

Also known as background lighting, this comes in the form of wall and ceiling lights and large table lamps. This lighting is very bright and white, and can seem cold and impersonal. It can be diffused by using dimmer switches or tinted tubes, which can accentuate room colours and complement the choice of floral arrangements. For example, if your room is decorated in blue, a blue tube could emphasize the mood that you are trying to create. It will do nothing for warmer colours such as red, however.

TASK LIGHTING

Used for particular purposes such as reading or writing. The lights are less white, but they are bright and used to channel light to a particular area. They are usually spotlights that can be altered by coloured bulbs to give off tints and therefore affect the mood of the room if used collectively. These lights benefit red, orange and yellow flowers but do nothing for blue ones.

△ *Yellow and pink flowers are very well-suited to candlelight.*

ACCENT LIGHTING OR SPOT LIGHTING

This lighting highlights specific parts of a room – pictures or architectural features such as arches or alcoves. It is a softer, yellower lighting and can be used effectively alone, creating a warm feeling but with sufficient light to see and accentuate. Warmer colours are best used in these circumstances to maintain their true colour and enhance their appearance.

CANDLE LIGHTING

This is very yellow and gives off little light, although a number of candles together can give substantial light to a room. The light is focused above the flame and therefore only illuminates that which is directly around it. The darkness above creates a soft, warm glow and this is why it is favoured to induce romantic feelings. Light shades of colour are best for this type of light effect. Yellows, oranges, pinks, peaches, limes and whites are all ideal in candlelight. Darker colours will disappear and it may seem that you have gaps in your arrangements.

02 gift bouquets

bouquets

The gift bouquet is not a recent phenomenon – it is something that goes back many, many years and was first referred to as a 'tussie-mussie', or nosegay. As far back as the 15th century, evidence of these bouquets were recorded as a 'tumose of flowrys or other herbys'. These tussie-mussies included many herbs for their fresh fragrance and the belief that they refreshed the head and stimulated the memory. Some even believed that they would be protected from illness or death by smelling these herbs and therefore avoid the germs that led to diseases such as the plague.

Bouquets reached their peak of popularity in Victorian England as fashionable accessories. As admirers combined them with the floral 'language of love', so they became known as 'word-posies', or 'articulated nosegays'. For example, simple messages of love were declared by bearing a small posy of red roses, just as they are today. Each flower conveyed a message, but if the recipient was unfamiliar with their meanings, the message could easily be misinterpreted.

There are many different interpretations of flowers and their properties. Below are some common examples.

Today we still regard posies as a powerful representation of love and protection, and we often use them for gifts and weddings. We usually send flowers to a loved one or to cheer up someone who is ill. The language of love as represented by flowers is still popular among brides today, as they look for symbols and messages to be included in their bouquets, as do loved ones choosing a funeral tribute.

In this section we show three styles of hand-tied bouquet: the open gift bouquet that is gift-wrapped in cellophane and a bubble of water; a modern hand-tied linear style; and the tight, hand-held, all-round posy often carried by brides.

FLOWERS AND THEIR MEANINGS

acacia – secret love
allspice – compassion
amaryllis – pride
anemone – unfading love
begonia – beware
bluebell – humility and everlasting love
bouquet of withered flowers – rejected love
bouvardia – enthusiasm
buttercup – childishness
carnation (red) – my heart aches for you
carnation (striped) – refusal/rejection

crocus – cheerfulness
cyclamen – unrequited love
daffodil – respect
dahlia – dignity/elegance
daisy – innocence
eucalyptus – protection
fern (maidenhair) – secret bond of love
forget-me-not – true love
freesia – trust and friendship
gardenia – purity/refinement
geranium – folly/stupidity
gypsophila – pure of heart/innocence
heather (white) – protection
iris – faith and wisdom

ivy – fidelity and friendship
lily (orange) – hatred
lily (white) – virginity and purity
magnolia – dignity
mistletoe – kiss me
myrtle – duty and affection
nasturtium – patriotism
pansy – thoughtful reflection
poppy – eternal sleep
rosemary – remembrance
salvia (blue) – I think of you
sunflower – loyalty

hand-tied in aqua pack

This design uses medium-sized flowers and contrasting foliage, tied using the spiral technique and gift-wrapped in cellophane with tissue paper and ribbon. The base is a cellophane 'bubble' filled with water. Before you start, prepare and assemble all your materials in neat piles. All foliage and thorns, etc. must be removed from the lower half of the stems, leaving them clear and clean from debris. Any lower branches on foliage must also be removed and placed in a separate pile to be used later on if possible.

Materials used:
- eucalyptus foliage • spray carnations • veronica • lilies • agapanthus • grass foliage • twine • ribbon • cellophane
- tissue paper

how to...

MAKE A HAND-TIED BOUQUET WITH A WATER-FILLED BASE

① Using eucalyptus foliage, find tall, straight stems and place the first straight down the centre of your palm. Hold your hand flat and use your thumb to secure the plant material. The second stem should be placed directly on top of the first, but slightly at an angle to the left. The third stem should rest on top of the first two stems, again at an angle slightly more to the left. By this stage the stems will want to move and swivel, therefore you must now begin to curl your fingers around the stems, almost closing your hand.

② Continue adding more and more stems in the same manner until you have a fistful. You will notice that as you have continued to apply materials at an angle in the same diagonal direction, the stems feel uniform, smooth and flow together naturally into a spiral.

③ Now add flower material in the same way as the foliage. Small buds of a light colour have been used here to add texture and help build shape. The stems of the flowers are placed in a diagonal direction, following the spiral of the foliage. The larger, more open buds are placed into the centre by pushing the stems through the centre point of the foliage.

④ Add purple veronica for more colour and texture. They are also long and thin, allowing for another shape and creating movement within the design, as your eye travels over the length of the flower head.

⑤ The main focal flowers are now added, giving depth of colour and dominance. The size of the flower head is very large, adding interest to the centre and edges. As the materials build up, it becomes harder to add material. It is possible to release your tight grip around the material, thus creating a hole in the centre and allowing a space for you to add further materials into. If your hand is aching, place the flowers down carefully lengthwise on a table and stretch out your hand and arm downwards towards your knee. This will allow the muscles to relax and the blood to flow more easily.

⑥ Adding more and more colour (purple agapanthus has been used here) builds up the mood of your bouquet and the shape becomes more pronounced. This is the time to use up any short lengths of foliage or flowers. Add them around the edge, bringing the colour downwards. Adding the grass helps the bouquet look bigger, drawing the eye outwards and creating movement.

⑦ Using a length of strong twine is best to secure the bouquet and tie it off. Find a length, fold it over, carry the loop around and tuck the ends through the loop. Pull the two ends tight through the loop and tie them off in a double knot.

⑧ At this point the bouquet should be secure and the stems cut all at the same point. The measurements of the bouquet should stand at two thirds above the tie point and one third below. After you have cut the stems, place the bouquet in a vase treated with flower food.

9 If you are wrapping the bouquet for a gift, the flowers should be set aside safely at this point while the gift wrap is prepared. The cellophane should now be prepared for the aqua pack, or 'bubble' of water. Cut two squares large enough to reach above the tie point of the flowers. Scrunch the cellophane up and around the base of the flowers, making sure that all of the stems are covered and that the cellophane reaches up equally around the flowers.

10 Secure with sticky tape and ribbon.

11 Cut two lengths of decorative gift-wrap and wrap these around the outside of the flowers and cellophane. Attach a pre-prepared bow and stand upright. Attach any gift cards or flower food and prepare a jug of water. Pour the water very slowly into the centre of the bouquet, allowing the 'bubble' of cellophane at the base to fill. Do not over-fill the bottom, as it may cause the bouquet to leak from the sides when held.

alternative design

This hand-held bouquet was made using the same spiral technique as the previous design, with small-scale flowers and foliage tied and finished with a trimming. Instead of starting with foliage, different coloured roses have been used, and viburnum berries added. The colours are soft and luxurious, the light and dark roses complementing each other, and the textures are romantic. Feathers and a dark, rich, velvet ribbon were included to add style and texture. These also emphasize the mood created by the colours, making it a dramatic and romantic bouquet.

tips

- Hold your bouquet tightly as you assemble it, but take care not to squash fragile stems. By loosening your grip, the materials will fall back onto to your fingers, leaving a gap in the centre to enable you to place additional material nearer the centre or remove and reposition stems.

- If you want to remove a stem that doesn't work, it is better to identify it from the bottom and push it up and out of the bouquet. You can then reach in over the top of the flowers and take it out once it protrudes from the others, making it easy to move and reposition. Never go directly into the bouquet from the top as you will damage the other materials.

- Do not forget how effective foliage can be and how it enhances your flowers and the outcome of the bouquet.

- Assemble all of your materials and gift wrap before you begin, so that everything is close to hand.

- Look for unusual wrappings and trimming to make your designs stylish and unique.

- Be aware of seasonal availability. Most flowers can be used for hand-tying, but it is especially lovely to see each season's flowers made up into arrangements.

- It may be effective to use the same type of flower for a particular look, but do not be afraid to experiment and explore different textures and colour combinations.

modern line gift bouquet

This modern bouquet is a limited arrangement of structural materials. It has a minimalist design in a linear style, consisting of few exotic blooms arranged with sculptural leaves. This design is a great opportunity to use exotics, as illustrated here, and try some unusual combinations. The same spiral technique is used as on previous pages, as you place materials in and around one another. This could be used for a wedding bouquet, a funeral tribute or a gift depending on the materials used and the gift-wrapping.

Materials used:
• steel grass • kniphofia • leucadendron • hypericum berries • monstera leaves • raffia

how to...

MAKE A MODERN LINE HAND-TIED BOUQUET

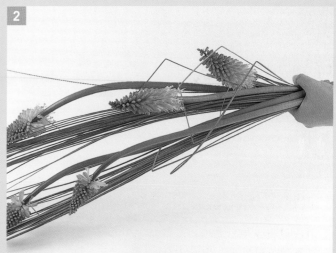

① Bunch the steel grass together in your hand. Bend over strands of grass randomly and fold them into the base of the arrangement, where the tie point in the hand will be. Hold the materials securely. If you are struggling to keep the materials together, tie with pot tape at the base before you continue.

② Place the smaller buds of kniphofia furthest away from the tie point where the hand holds the grass. Stagger the five flowers evenly apart from one another. Hold the materials securely. Again, if you are struggling to keep the materials together, tie with pot tape at the base before you continue.

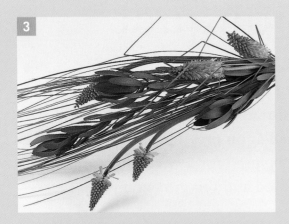

③ Place the three leucadendron blooms lower and towards the base, using the largest of the blooms nearest the base. By using the largest blooms here, the size and intensity of the colour help with the recession and make the bouquet look longer, as the colour and size decrease towards the edges.

④ Add one cluster of hypericum berries at the base to continue the colour and to add another texture. These berries blend in well with the other materials and add more interest and focus at the tie point.

⑤ Placing large leaves at the base balances the height created by the grass, and helps with the proportion of the arrangement. Finish off by tying with a suitable material – in this case, the natural straw raffia bow was appropriate for the tropical flowers.

ALTERNATIVE DESIGNS

Winter wedding: Red and green colours, e.g. hibiscus, equisetum (snake) grass, zantedeschia (cala lilies), euphorbia fulgens and leucospermum (protea).

Spring gift: White and yellow colours, e.g. salix fragilis (pussy willow), eremurus (sword lily), iris (Madonna), genista (broom) and ranunculus.

tips

- Choose your materials carefully, ensuring long, strong stems are used.

- Keep it simple and use just one or two colours to make the outcome more dramatic.

- If the leaves are large, the bow should also be an appropriate size to balance them out. Ensure that each material has different textures.

03 | arrangements

creating arrangements

There are many sources available to enable even the most inexperienced flower arranger to make attractive designs. Market stalls, shops, supermarkets and importers are all increasing their stock and flowers are becoming very much part of our everyday lives, instead of a luxury item or something just for special occasions. As a result, good quality materials are now much more easy to obtain.

Containers have developed over the years and the choices are unlimited, with everything from baskets to aluminum pots and ceramics now available. Interior designers are incorporating structural designs as part of their work, and our role as a florist or flower arranger is vital to their overall success.

In this section we have made a selection of both traditional and modern arrangements to give you the opportunity to choose accordingly for each occasion that you are designing for. There are many other designs in floristry, but we have chosen these as we feel that they are used most frequently, and will also give you the skills to enable you to adapt them as and where necessary.

▽ *Containers are available in all shapes and sizes. Always make sure that you secure your base safely, with pot tape if necessary.*

symmetrical front-facing

This arrangement is in a classic triangular shape which can be made to suit the proportions and scale of any setting, and it remains one of the most popular for giving visual impact at functions and events. As a pair to frame a doorway or either side of an altar or podium, and singly to accentuate a corner or provide interest against a plain wall, the pleasing symmetry of this arrangement will show off even the simplest materials used in its creation.

Materials used:
• deep tray or bowl • floral foam • pot tape • ruscus and viburnum foliages • lisianthus • roses • lilies
• chrysanthemums • tuberose

how to...

CREATE A CLASSIC TRIANGULAR ARRANGEMENT

This example, designed to sit on a pedestal at the front of a church, for instance, demonstrates how a simple selection of summer blooms can be transformed into an elegant and formal display which will complement the most ornate of surroundings.

① **Soak some floral foam and secure with pot tape, ensuring that the foam is at least 5 cm (2 in) above the rim of the dish. It is important to use enough foam to accommodate the amount of stems being used in the design.**

▷

② Make an outline triangular shape with long-stemmed foliage, with all stems appearing to radiate from the centre of the design. The lowest pieces at either side should be placed into the foam at a slight upwards angle to allow foliage to fall softly over the edge of the dish.

③ Add more greenery to the centre and front edges to form the basis for the design, and also minimize the need to fill in too much later on.

tip

To achieve the required three-dimensional effect which ensures that the design does not look as if it is falling forwards in the container, the background materials need to be angled backwards slightly, giving an impression of depth.

④ Using your foliage as a background guide, place long stemmed, pointed flowers (in this case lisianthus) to echo the outline shape and create definition of form.

⑤ Establish a focal line with your choicest materials, using an odd number such as seven or nine flowers and graduating them from the top to the base of the design.

⑦ Finally, fill in with less expensive materials such as chrysanthemum sprays to give recession and ensure that there are no gaps in the design. However, it is essential to avoid a compacted centre by excessive filling in and to remember that there is a need for some 'positive space' between materials. The maxim 'knowing when to stop' really applies here, and will come with practice and experience.

⑥ Begin to fill out the shape with more focal materials, varying heights and depths so that each bloom is shown to its best advantage.

alternative design

This contemporary form has been achieved by using a selection of natural and dried materials in a moss-covered container. Height is attained with stems of twisted willow and pampas grass, and the focal area is dominated by the preserved sunflowers.

tips

• If the design is large-scale and will require four or more foam blocks in the container to hold all the materials, it is advisable to secure a net of chicken wire over them before commencing the design. This will prevent the foam from breaking apart and the arrangement becoming unstable.

• Additional height can be attained by using foam-filled plastic or tin tubes (available from floristry wholesalers) mounted onto sticks and inserted into the container.

all-round posy bowl

This versatile arrangement is suitable for many occasions and venues, from a small gift item to sit on a friend's coffee table, to a large urn arrangement in the centre of a hotel foyer, or as one of a weekly contract order for all the dining tables in a restaurant. A candle placed in the centre gives an added dimension to the design and, when accessorized with seasonal materials (for example, decorative eggs and gingham ribbon bows for Easter, or cinnamon sticks and pine cones for Christmas), you can see how this simple form can be adapted and enhanced.

Materials used:
- plastic posy bowl dish • floral foam • pot tape • pillar candle • 71mm stub wires • decorative bullion wire
- ruscus • snowberry (symphoricarpos) • roses • gerberas • hypericum

how to...

CREATE A POSY BOWL

① Immerse the floral foam in water for one or two minutes until thoroughly soaked. Cut to the required shape and size to fit the bowl, allowing for a height of approximately 2.5 cm (1 in) of foam above the dish, and secure using pot tape.

▷

② Bend several stub wires to make long pins and attach to the candle using pot tape.

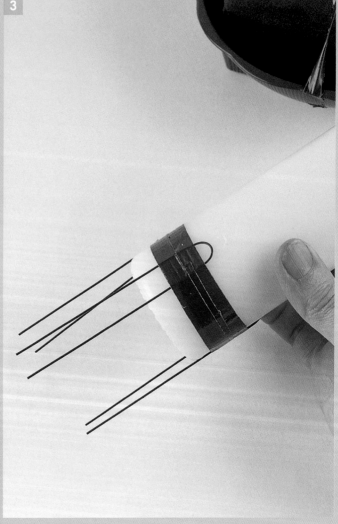

③ Three or four pins evenly spaced around the candle should be sufficient, but make sure that they are long enough to anchor the candle safely onto the foam base.

4

④ Place the candle securely into the centre of the foam, ensuring a good anchorage with the pins so there is no danger of it falling over.

⑤ Cut sprigs of foliage (ruscus) and place at five intervals around the lower outside edge of the bowl, angling the stems upwards into the foam so that the foliage lies over the sides, concealing the plastic dish. Add three sprigs around the candle at the centre.

5

▷

⑥ With contrasting foliage (snowberry), place five smaller sprigs in between the first outer ones and three more to the centre.

⑦ Using the foliage outline as your guide, place focal roses at the same three central and five outer points on top of the greenery.

⑧ Occasionally some materials, such as gerberas, need some extra support to straighten up and strengthen their stems before use in a design. This can be done by introducing a 71mm stub wire approximately 5 cm (2 in) below the flower head and feeding it up inside the stem until it anchors inside the receptacle. Stop at this point – it should not protrude out of the centre of the bloom. Cut the stem and wire together at the appropriate height for your design.

⑨ To give some recessional quality to the design, place three rounded, shaped flowers deep into the central area around the candle base. This will also help to cover the foam from view and minimize the need for too much filling in later.

⑩ Continue to build up the design by adding more materials in the form of secondary flowers and foliage around the focal placements.

⑪ When the arrangement is completed, add some decorative elements such as pearl-headed pins into the focal rose centres and twisted bullion wire strands amongst the fresh material, which will sparkle when the candle is lit.

tips

- When wetting floral foam, insert a long stub wire straight through several times and leave submerged until any bubbling ceases. This will ensure that the centre of the foam is completely soaked.

- Whenever candles are included in an arrangement, safety instructions must be attached warning the user not to leave it unattended when lit – particularly if decorative and possibly flammable items are also part of the design.

- Plastic candle-cups are available to buy for use with long dinner-table candles, as an alternative to the wire pins shown here.

tank vase arrangements

The characteristics of modern design include using colour and texture in abundance. These components should be bold and dramatic, and closely mirrored by the space and form. Containers play a huge part in modern design, as they are integral to the overall look – the tank vases used here are a good example of this.

Modern arrangements are suited to this container. Glass is hard and transparent, allowing a florist to explore a variety of textures and themes. In the designs shown here, we have used materials to decorate both inside and outside. It illustrates how just one simple vase can be used in a variety of ways to create a multitude of designs.

Vase 1: **Hand-tied**

Materials used:
• aspidistra leaves
• ruscus
• freesia
• roses
• aster
• lisianthus

The vase is lined with aspidistra leaves and water poured into the base. The compact hand-tied bouquet in a triad colour scheme (three colours at equal distance on the colour wheel: orange/violet/green) is securely positioned inside. Round-shaped flowers are used to make the hand-tied appear even more circular in style, and this complements the square vase.

Vase 2: **Vegetation**

Materials used:

- roses
- gypsophila
- anthirium
- spray carnations
- fern
- kiwi fruit
- grapes
- beans

This modern arrangement is a collection of materials with an emphasis on texture. The vase has been camouflaged with green beans to add another element, and disguise the hard glass. A variety of textures have been applied but the arrangement is kept just white and green, to make it simple and soft. A candle has been placed in the centre to illustrate that it could be used as a centrepiece for a dining room table. This can be viewed all round and different materials have been placed in groups around the candle. The roses extend upwards to match the depth of the vase, and help balance the other materials. The fruit and vegetables in this design contribute an interesting originality and sense of humour.

Vase 3: **Reach for the sky**

Materials used:
- twigs
- gladioli
- roses
- anthurium
- fatsia japonica leaves

The vase is lined with fatsia japonica leaves, the veins on the leaves showing clearly through the glass to add another dimension to the arrangement. Gladioli, tall and proud in the centre, are protected by twigs that reach upwards and out of the arrangement. A triad colour scheme (three colours at equal distance on the colour wheel: orange/violet/green) is used.
A selection of flower materials are arranged around the base in a repetitive pattern, and the addition of fatsia japonica leaves flop over the edge to soften the look.

Vase 4: **Haywire**

Materials used:
- anthurium
- aluminium wire
- kermit
  chrysanthemums
- agapanthus buds
- coloured beads

This inspirational design is made simply with florist's glue, aluminium wire and beads. A complementary colour scheme is used (opposite on the colour wheel: red-violet/yellow-green), two colours keeping the design uncomplicated. The wire is uncoiled and in sections wound around a pencil to produce a corkscrew effect. The beads and flowers are glued on individually and in clusters at various intervals, before being carefully squashed into the vase. The flowers are sprayed with water and flower preservative. This is a dramatic design showing that floristry can be theatre too! Have fun with your materials and play with ideas.

Vase 5: The sphere

Vase 6: Lemon and lime

Materials used:
- roses
- ivy leaves
- decorative pins
- foam ball

A very contemporary look has been created here as we play with negative and positive space. The circle within a square plays on form and shape. Which do you think is more dominant, the circle or the square? The colour scheme is simple, bold and adds to the drama of the display. This colour scheme is near-complementary (or opposite-but-one to the main colour: red-orange/green). This is an all-round arrangement for a modern setting.

Materials used:
- lemons
- limes
- kermit and yellow chrysanthemums
- coloured foam

The vase is filled with lemon and lime-coloured foam to add light to the arrangement and support the fruit and flowers. Alternate slices of lemons and limes line the glass to great visual effect. A row of flowers is placed into the foam and the pattern is repeated. These are analogous colours as they are next to each other on the colour wheel, working well together. This design can be viewed from all round and again could be used as a centrepiece on a dining room table.

Vase 7: **Christmas boxes**

Materials used:
- silver sprayed pinecones
- white snowball decorations
- beaded twigs
- decorative parcels
- roses
- carnations
- foam
- feathers

The vase was camouflaged with double-sided tape and white feathers. Beaded glittery twigs add height, texture and movement in this design. Christmas balls and boxes are grouped front and back amongst the flowers to make this a double-sided arrangement. This could be described as a monochromatic colour scheme (one colour and white). The hard glass cube is almost invisible, but the feathers enhance the textures used and the blue boxes help to repeat the shape of the cube vase. A seasonal design for a shelf or mantelpiece.

modern line window

This design is influenced by the modern European styles. There are clear sections of colours and textures, and this technique is known as 'clumping' or 'grouping' materials together into sections. They are normally used for a window ledge, mantelpiece or shelf area. Once the style has been mastered, the materials can be changed to create topical and original design. For example, at Halloween you could have a display of orange and black colours with accessories added such as pumpkins and spiders. Harvest time could be a display with vegetables and flowers.

Materials used:
- rectangular container • floral foam • stapler • oil or leaf shine • aspidistra leaves • roses • poppy seed heads
- carnation blooms • anthuriums • fatsia japonica leaves

how to...

CREATE A WINDOW ARRANGEMENT

The modern line arrangement uses groups of textures and dramatic use of space by varying the material heights. Nothing radiates from the central point as it would with a traditional arrangement; each material is dominant in its own right. Choose your materials carefully to ensure that the emphasis is either on colour, space or texture or a combination of all three.

① The container for this arrangement is integral to the design and has been chosen for its muted colour and rough texture. This will complement the arrangement well, as it is a dominant feature in the design. Place soaked floral foam into the container and secure with florists' tape if your materials are particularly heavy or bulky.

② Wash your aspidistra leaves carefully and shine them with a glossy oil (vegetable oil or pre-prepared florist's leaf shine). Curl and twist the leaves into the desired shape and fix with staples.

③ Add your leaves to the foam. These play a large part in the design as they show colour and texture over a large surface area. Movement can be created by allowing the shape and veining of the leaves to point in different directions.

④ The roses are a striking colour against the dark green and work well in contrast to the swirly, twisted, angled leaves. Place the roses in a line, making them look rigid in comparison to the leaves.

⑤ Use poppy seed heads for their size and muted colour. They add another element to the design against the soft, silky, bright red roses. Place them at different angles in order to move away from the strong line of roses.

▷

⑥ **Add carnation blooms to continue the pattern of colour, increasing the texture by clumping the fluffy heads together low down into the foam. Anthiriums accentuate the colour scheme and add another texture in comparison to their neighbour, being flat and shiny. This material rises slightly above the previous material, creating movement within the design.**

⑦ **Fatsia japonica leaves, large in area and flat and bold, bring a dramatic end to the arrangement. The design now flows from one end to the other, beginning and ending with leaves.**

ALTERNATIVE MATERIALS

Most materials could be used for this arrangement. All foliage species can be just as attractive, and bright, bold designs made with unusual colour schemes and varieties are very dramatic.

tips

- Always use fresh materials.

- Some materials may require wiring for support. These must be hidden, camouflaged or made decorative, and be integral to the design.

- Use structural materials, carefully chosen for texture, colour, size and shape.

traditional long low

The soft lines and graceful shaping of this arrangement enhances a table dressed for a dinner party or wedding breakfast, a church windowsill or altar rail, a mantelpiece or console table. In fact, there are so many situations in which its diamond outline works that it has become one of the most versatile designs in a florist's portfolio. It has even gained a place in the funeral tribute catalogue as a double-ended spray.

Materials used:
- plastic tray • floral foam • pot tape • plastic pin holder • putty fixative • ruscus • snowberry (symphoricarpos)
- hydrangea • chrysanthemum blooms • lilies • tuberose • roses

how to...

CREATE A LONG, LOW ARRANGEMENT

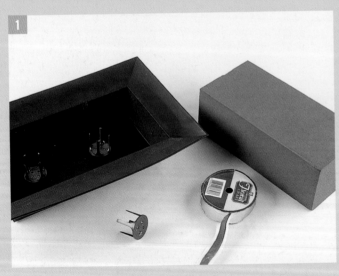

① The equipment required for this design is minimal and cost-effective so, as the container is not seen at all, a simple plastic tray large enough to accommodate a single block of floral foam is really all that's required. The plastic pin holder or 'frog' pictured, which is stuck into the base with a putty-like fix, will give some added stability to this large-scale 'top-table' version for a wedding.

② Soak the foam thoroughly in water and place in the container, securing with pot tape widthways. Securing it in this way means that there will be ample space left in the centre of the foam to insert the semi-woody stems of lilies and hydrangea.

③ Place the folliage equally at each end and side of the design to achieve the diamond outline shape.

④ Carry the foliage across the centre of the foam also, for added definition.

⑤ Using long, slender elements, the shape is echoed with tuberose and a focal line of roses carried from one end, through the centre, to the other. The height should be approximately equal to one of the side pieces and no higher so that, if placed on the centre of a table, guests are still able to see and talk to each other easily.

⑥ Introduce larger recessional blooms throughout the focal area, making sure that the choice roses are not overwhelmed and hidden.

⑦ Place further focal flowers in parallel lines across the main focal line, and add lily buds for an accent colour and shape.

⑧ For contrasting colour and texture, add sprigs of hydrangea placed low down amongst the other flowers. These also help to fill in any gaps so that the foam is covered completely, which is very important when a design is able to be viewed at very close quarters.

tips

- Position three long, tapered candles at varying heights in the centre, for a design to be used on the table at an evening dinner party.

- By adding trailing foliage and extending the flowers on one side of the design, it can be positioned on the edge of a top table at a function as a cascading design, providing interest and decoration to an otherwise plain tablecloth edge.

- When making this as a mantelpiece design it must, of course, be predominantly front facing, but remember to retain its graceful line by keeping the centre low. This is even more important if a mirror or painting is positioned above, when the arrangement should extend only high enough to overlap the frame.

04 wedding designs

wedding flowers

When taking on a commission to provide wedding flowers, it is your job as a florist to make a bride feel that choosing them is something to be enjoyed, and not a chore. It is essential to get to know your bride to establish her likes and dislikes. Set up a consultation with her early on, and establish dates, styles, budgets, numbers, etc. It is useful to collect pictures from magazines and to show her some photos of your previous work. You will then need to provide costings and delivery times and confirm materials and colours. It can be very difficult costing up designs, as prices change from season to season, but you should be aware of this and be able to warn the bride of price rises and difficulties in obtaining certain materials. Lastly, you should finalize any last-minute changes, ask for swatches of material to compare flower shades to, and confirm payments, delivery times and addresses.

There may be more consultations, such as joining the bride at the venue, should she wish you to decorate it, and meeting with the bride's mother and/or bridesmaids to discuss their flowers. When designing for small bridesmaids, always check their ages and be very careful with the materials that you use. It would not be wise, for example, to add small berries into their designs for fear of them being eaten or squashed into pretty dresses. Weight should also be considered carefully, as a young bridesmaid may not be able to manage something that is uncomfortable to hold.

Brides nowadays have a very good idea of what they want and seem to be fairly knowledgeable of the flowers available to them. It is best to make absolutely sure that the bride knows what she is getting – show her pictures of the flowers for confirmation that you are talking about the same thing, and suggest alternatives if you think the initial choice unsuitable. Remember, it is your work that is going on display and it will be an advert of your professionalism and capabilities. If you do not agree with the bride's choice, you should try to gently persuade her otherwise.

Bridal fashions have varied over the years, and we have moved from gathered posies to wired bouquets, from wired bouquets back to hand-tied posies, and now we are seeing the trend swing again towards wired work. Whatever the bride chooses, however, the design must always suit the

△ *Always keep the bride informed if the costings change at all.*

△ *Seasonal flowers are cheaper and easier to get hold of.*

occasion, and it is your job to ensure that the correct style is achieved. This is another reason why you need to meet with the bride to ascertain the shape, size and style of her dress and venue, be it formal or informal, traditional or modern.

At times like this it is lovely to include the 'language of love' that the Victorians used by conveying secret messages through flower and foliage selection. There are many myths and superstitions connected with weddings, and the most well-known one in the western world is that the bride should wear something old, something new, something borrowed and something blue.

Others are:

Russia: Never give a knife as a gift – it is considered unlucky.

Europe: It is unlucky for the groom to see his bride in her wedding outfit before the ceremony.

Ireland: If the bride has lavender in her bouquet it is considered good luck and will bring good fortune and make all her wishes come true.

UK: It is considered bad luck to use red and white flowers together, as it symbolizes 'blood and bandages'.

Spain: If the groom's best man cuts off a piece of the groom's tie and keeps it, he will marry soon after.

Japan: Brides must change outfits several times in order to bring good luck.

India: Mango leaves are given to bless the marriage with sons.

(Source: *The Superstitious Bride* by Rosalind Franklin, Diggory Press, 2005)

◁ *Make sure that you discuss the colour scheme well in advance.*

fully-wired wedding bouquet

This design is probably the most technically difficult of all bridal bouquets to make, requiring not only a good level of wiring and construction skill but also the confidence and speed to be able to achieve a complex and beautiful piece of work which justifies the necessarily high cost. With the huge popularity of natural-style tied bouquets in recent years, fewer florists have developed the skills required to be able to offer this design. As always, though, the pendulum of fashion is swinging back in favour of more traditional shapes, albeit with a contemporary edge in terms of accessories and trimmings. The classic 'shower' or 'teardrop' style, which can only be achieved with wiring, is making its resurgence in bridal magazines, which tend to inspire most brides.

Materials used:
• silver reel wire and rose wires • 90mm stub wires • floral tape • roses • gerberas • tuberose • alstroemeria • ivy

how to...

CREATE A FULLY-WIRED WEDDING BOUQUET

A few of the popular misconceptions about fully-wired designs include assumptions that they must be heavy and cannot last very long, as the materials are not in water. In fact the opposite is true, as the gauges of wires used are extremely light, producing a design with a handle which is compact and comfortable to hold – with the added bonus that there is no danger of drips to mark a delicate fabric. Also, the florist tape which is used to cover all the wires not only ensures a smooth finish, but effectively seals moisture into the flower and foliage stems, so that even on a hot day the bouquet will remain fresh certainly throughout the ceremony and photographs, and probably on into the reception as well. This is more than can be said for some hand-tied posies, which can be bulky to carry and soon wilt in the heat of the day, unless the stems are cut and put back into water at the reception. The following design is a sumptuous, tear-drop version of sweetly-scented summer blooms and garden foliage in soft shades of pink and cream, perfectly complementing a full-skirted gown.

① **Begin by wiring natural, trailing units of foliage on to long 90mm stub wires, using silver wires to secure and covering with floral tape.**

② Make units of one, two or three leaves by first individually wiring on to silver rose wires, and then mounting in groups or singly on to long 90mm stubs. These will be useful later on for filling gaps in the centre and the trail of the bouquet.

③ Next, wire all the flowers individually on to silver rose wires using the single-leg technique, and then mount on to long 90mm stub wires, taping securely to lock moisture into the stems and cover all the mechanics.

④ Ensure that all fresh material is neatly and securely wired, taped and carefully laid out on your work surface, ready for the construction of the design. It's a good idea to mist all materials with tepid water and allow them to 'rest' for a few minutes before handling again, to retain freshness and minimize damage to leaves and petals

⑤ Begin assembling the trail of the bouquet first, by taking several of the natural foliage units and attaching the silver reel wire, making two or three secure twists of the wire each time you add more units and widening the shape slightly as you do so. Remember to combine flowers and foliage so that colour and form flows through and up into the main focal area of the design.

⑥ When the trail is beginning to take shape, create a handle by bending the wires acutely at an angle which is comfortable to hold and will allow space for you to begin forming the focal area of the bouquet.

⑦ Using foliage units, arrange the outline of the bouquet so that it balances the trail, which should be roughly two thirds in length of the overall completed design. Continue to build the design by combining flowers and foliage through the centre and at the outer edges, placing these on top of the outline foliage units, and binding securely with reel wire.

tip

Be careful to keep the binding point in one place, as this maintains the stability of the bouquet whilst you are constructing it.

⑧ In this design the focal line of roses is carried through from the base of the trail to the top, giving a defined form and streak of colour. It also contributes balance and harmony to the overall design, whether viewed from above or face-on.

⑨ The contrasting shape and texture of the gerberas provide a strong recessional quality to the main body of this design, with their rounded forms, flawless petals and striking deep brown centres.

⑩ It is essential to trim the wires regularly throughout construction in a graduated way. This will minimize the weight and create a slim, comfortable handle for the bride to hold.

⑪ All mechanics must be covered neatly with floral tape, making sure that there are no sharp wires protruding which might damage the bride's dress or hands.

⑫ **Even though the back of the bouquet is only going to be visible to the bride, it is both considerate and professional to finish the handle with a covering of luxury ribbon and a pretty bow for a keepsake.**

ALTERNATIVE SELECTIONS

For most brides, the dominant factor in choosing her flowers tends to be colour, with perhaps a favourite flower requested and the rest left to the floral designer to decide. This makes sense in most cases, where the bride knows little about flowers and allows the florist to choose what's best at market on the day, according to their given budget. However, increasingly nowadays, a theme is carried throughout all of the arrangements and the floral designs are a prominent feature of it. Here are some examples:

Scented theme: Teardrop of gardenias, stephanotis and lily-of-the-valley – a heady, creamy-white selection evocative of 1950s-style bouquets and fashion icon brides such as Grace Kelly and Audrey Hepburn.

Exotic: Modern line design of dendrobium orchids, cala lilies, and long bear grass or plaited palm leaves.

Cottage garden: Trailing shower bouquet of waxflower, lisianthus, spray roses and freesias in mixed colours, combining perfume and texture reminiscent of countryside hedgerows.

tips

- Flowers and foliage should be appropriately conditioned and allowed to drink in a cool, shady place for at least 24 hours before starting to wire.

- Avoid using dyed material in bridal bouquets, and remove stamens from lilies so as to avoid accidental staining occurring to fabrics and dresses.

- Request a swatch of material from the bride and bridesmaid's gowns for accurate colour matching when buying flowers.

victorian posy on foam

Popular among the Victorians, these posies often carried messages of love via the hidden language of flowers. These traditional posies feature tightly packed materials in rings of colour, and are usually held by bridesmaids. Usually there are at least five rings of texture and colour, one being the main focal flower followed by at least four concentric circles, each one tightly massed. They are considered a traditional design, but a modern slant can be incorporated by using clashing, vibrant colours.

Materials used:
• posy holder • red and orange roses • chrysanthemums • hypericum berries • bullion wire • ivy leaves

how to...

CREATE A VICTORIAN POSY ON FOAM

① The materials used for this design are small and the stems are strong. The posy holder shown is normally for silk flowers, but can be used for these designs as well. The fresh (or silk) flowers could be secured into the dried foam with florists glue, but we are using the traditional method by using a posy holder with wet foam. This way, the flowers are carefully inserted into the foam and they are able to drink water and remain fresh, lasting all day.

② A Victorian posy should have clear bands of colours and textures. A rose should be placed first as the central flower, with all others placed at angles around it. The rose should be inserted carefully into the foam, at least 1 cm (0.5 in) to be secure.

③ Lime green chrysanthemums have been chosen for their texture and colour. They are a similar shape and should be closely packed in. Place the second layer slightly lower than the first flower and at an angle, pointing outwards.

④ Hypericum berries are used to contrast with the previous colours and add another texture and size element. The berries are a mixture of high- and low-placed on the stem and these add depth to the design when they are placed into the foam. They should be placed lower than the previous layer, with the higher buds on the stems protruding upwards towards the chrysanthemums.

⑤ Place orange roses underneath the berries, as a contrast to their size and colour. The roses are bold, and their colour luxurious.

⑥ Wire your ivy leaves for support and anchorage, and place them around the edge to finish off the design and to add another layer of colour and texture. The ivy is variegated and the white flecks add light to the design. Place them at least 2.5 cm (1 in) into the design, pointing downwards to trail over the hand and cover up the handle.

⑦ As a finishing touch, red bullion wire adds a delicate texture and the colour brings the red down from the top to the bottom. Wind the wire around a pencil five or six times and cut to be inserted at least 2.5 cm (1 in) into the foam.

ALTERNATIVE SELECTIONS

Other good flowers to use include sedum, gypsophila, heather, spray roses, wax flowers, viburnum, hebe, carnations and spray carnations. This arrangement can also be made by hand-tying the materials or wiring each material and binding each circle together.

tips

- If all the circles are created using large materials, the bouquet is likely to be very heavy to hold. Use smaller flowers and foliage for a more delicate result.

- You must be careful not to overload the foam, as it has a small capacity and will only hold a few flowers, or those with thin stems.

- Do not use flowers that are flat, i.e. gerberas and some chrysanthemums. They will make the bouquet dip, the shape distort and the area around the flower can be hard to fill, making the design at risk of showing gaps.

- A frill of lace was traditionally used around the outside, and can enhance your design by making it more authentic.

traditional corsage

On any formal occasion there can be no lovelier accompaniment for a lady's outfit than a complementary spray of fresh flowers on her collar, wrist or handbag. The distinctive kite shape of this design is echoed in many other floristry forms – for instance, front-facing arrangements, teardrop bridal bouquets and single-ended sprays – with stems appearing to radiate from a central point to achieve the balance and symmetry required.

Materials used:
• silver rose wires • floral tape • silver reel wire • roses • hypericum • smoke bush leaves • decorative pin to fix

how to...

CREATE A TRADITIONAL CORSAGE

① **Single-leg mount all the material in individual and double units on silver wires, and bind with floral tape.**

② Beginning with the smallest leaves, establish a binding point using silver reel wire. Be sure to allow enough room between the top of the spray and the binding area to be able to create the main triangular-shaped area of the design.

③ Add further material to form the outline, binding tightly several times to secure.

④ Begin to build the central area of the spray using secondary and focal flowers, as well as single leaves to fill in where necessary.

▷

⑤ Gradually widen the outline to form a triangular shape and introduce the final focal elements.

⑥ Make the 'return' or lower point of the corsage by placing leaves vertically, face-forwards against the spray and then bending back to form a rim of foliage which will give a neat edge and conceal the binding area from view. Trim the wires to form a neat stem and bind with floral tape. Provide a pin to allow the wearer to attach it to their outfit.

ALTERNATIVE SELECTIONS

The possible variations on this design in terms of colour and materials are endless depending on season, occasion and outfit. However, roses are always a good first choice for the focal element, as they come in such an infinite variety of shades that it is hard to imagine any colour of outfit which could not be matched or contrasted by some variety. Alternatively, a cream or white colour scheme will co-ordinate well with anything, and the addition of attractive foliage will always prevent a design from being too bland or monotone.

tips

- A small magnet can be bound into the stem as an alternative for attaching to delicate fabric, although people with certain medical conditions are not advised to wear these.

- This design can be sewn on to ribbon to attach to the wrist, waist or a handbag as an attractive and unusual accessory, particularly when the outfit being worn is sheer or strapless.

- As lightness of construction is paramount, only bind materials after two or three units are placed in position and not after each one.

rose buttonhole

This classic design is still the most popular men's buttonhole for any formal occasion, in particular at weddings where it is a very popular choice for the bridegroom's party. Its simple elegance adds an understated but stylish touch and, with the vast range of rose varieties and colours now being grown commercially, it can easily be co-ordinated to match the bridal flowers. Seasonal alternatives are very easy to create, making this an extremely versatile design.

Materials used:
• single rose • 90mm stub wires • silver rose wires • floral tape • pearl-headed pin

how to...

MAKE A ROSE BUTTONHOLE

① **Cut off the rose head, leaving approximately 2.5 cm (1 in) of stem and insert the stub wire until it just enters the calyx (rounded base underneath the rose). Secure by passing a silver wire through it and twisting around the stem and stub wire.**

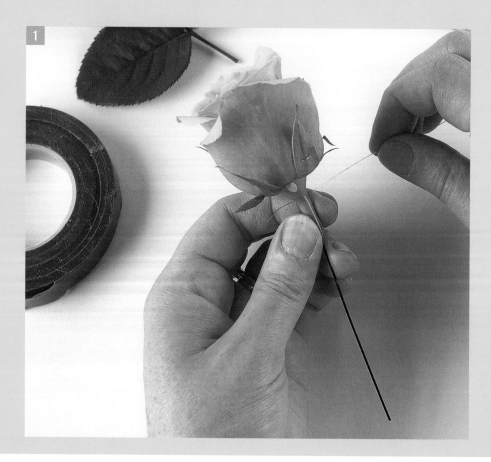

② Cover the stem and wires with floral tape, stretching the tape and twirling the stem in your fingers to give a neat finish.

③ Select a trefoil of leaves from discarded rose stems, ensuring that they are undamaged and well-shaped. Holding the trefoil with the reverse side facing you, make a small stitch with a silver wire, about two thirds of the way up, across the vein at the back of the leaf. Pull the wires down parallel to the stem and secure in a single leg mount. Wire the remaining leaves in the same way and tape the wire stem to cover.

④ Position your rose on the trefoil, making sure that the top third of the centre leaf is visible for good visual balance. Tape the stems together neatly and securely to cover all mechanics. This will produce a smooth finish, ensuring that the wearer's clothing cannot be damaged by any loose wires. Finish by inserting a pearl-headed pin at an angle into the taped stem, so that the wearer can attach the buttonhole to their lapel.

tips

① (a–b) Roses are generally sold with the outer, bud-protecting petals (known as nursery or weather petals) still attached. These are sometimes attractive enough to leave intact, but often detract from the overall beauty of the bloom. They can be simply removed by gently pulling away from the base of the flower head.

② (a–b) To prevent the bloom from opening too quickly, particularly in very hot weather, the sepals can be pinned lightly against the rose head using tiny pins made from silver wires. This offers some 'resistance' to the petals as they try to open, without preventing it all together.

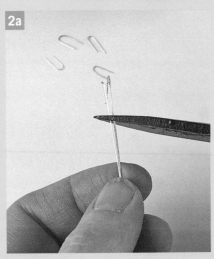

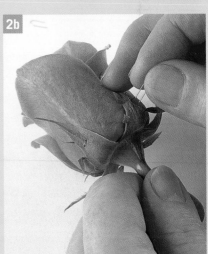

ALTERNATIVE SELECTIONS

Most rose varieties are, of course, available all year round, but there are many ways to ring the changes by the use of seasonal foliage and berries as well as incorporating unusual accessories such as feathers and beads. Here are just a few examples:

Autumnal: Hypericum, copper beech, oak leaves, wired acorn cups, Michaelmas daisy

Christmas: Floral glitter on petals, sequin strands, mistletoe sprigs, holly berries, ivy leaves, larkspur twiglets

Summer: Ribbon bows in gingham, organza or satin, crystal drops on wires, gypsophila, wax flower

alternative designs

▷ The addition of a button chrysanthemum, snowberry and variegated garden foliage transforms this buttonhole into a country-style sprig, whilst the pearl-headed pin placed in the centre of the rose retains a touch of luxury.

◁ Two roses present a more elaborate design, perhaps for the groom or father of the bride. Here, the contrasting colours and velvet texture of the blooms are offset by the tiny blue-black viburnum berries.

△◁ Moving right away from the traditional, these unusual and sculptural designs demonstrate how diverse and unique a simple buttonhole can be, when form and shape are imaginatively combined.

carnation buttonhole

The tradition of providing a buttonhole for every guest has waned somewhat over the years, with couples feeling less obligated by convention. However, for those who still want to honour at least some of their wedding party with a flower in their buttonhole, the simple, blousy form of a single carnation bloom is still a popular and affordable choice. They come in an infinite variety of hues, but the newer lime greens or the traditional pure whites will be guaranteed not to clash with anyone's outfit on the day.

Materials used:
• single carnation • gypsophila • 90mm stub wire • silver rose wires • floral tape • pearl-headed pin

how to...

CREATE A CARNATION BUTTONHOLE

The archetypal choice of foliage was always asparagus fern, but in latter days anything from leather leaf to gypsophila has been paired with carnations to provide a complementary foil.

① Wire and tape three individual pieces of gypsophila for placing around the carnation.

② Cut the carnation head, leaving approximately 2.5 cm (1 in) of stem, and push stub wire up and through the centre of the bloom.

③ Make a small hook and pull it back down into the flower head until anchored securely and out of sight.

④ Trim the wire and arrange each piece of gypsophila around the bloom, taping securely into place.

⑤ **Ensure that all wires are taped for a smooth finish, and to ensure no damage to fingers or fabrics.**

⑥ **Add a pearl-headed pin so that the wearer can attach the buttonhole to their clothing with ease.**

▷ *An alternative design can be made in the same way using three leather leaves and a different coloured carnation.*

informal boutonnière

Boutonnières are simply a collection of materials used for a lapel. These are unisex and the materials are normally a collection from the wedding flowers, so that all the guests blend in well. These are much more elaborate than a buttonhole and are normally used for more important members of the wedding party such as the groom, the best man and senior members of the family. The materials are gathered in at one tie point and secured with silver reel wire.

Materials used:
- florists' tape • wire • gladioli • ivy leaves • Japanese anemone seed heads • bupleurum
- variegated foliage

how to...

CREATE A BOUTONNIÈRE

Boutonnières can be suggested for guests instead of the more formal and traditional corsage. They are simple and cheap to make, and some lovely designs can be made with just a few materials and accessories.

① **Assemble your materials ready for use. The materials must be in excellent condition and prepared with care, as some are fragile and delicate. Wire up the materials for use and place to one side.**

② The gladioli should be wired using a double leg mount. All wires should then be taped with florists' tape.

③ Begin placing your materials together, using one binding point and with a large, flat leaf as the base.

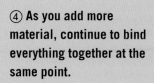

④ As you add more material, continue to bind everything together at the same point.

⑤ Build up the arrangement with a variety of interesting materials that compliment one another in shape, size and colour.

⑥ Ensure that all wires are covered with florists' tape and add a couple of decorative pearl-headed pins to secure the arrangement to a lapel.

tips

• Handle the flowers and foliage carefully and place them on to a clean surface.

• Store away from any light and draughts.

• Wrap in a box laid with tissue paper.

circlet headdress

Circlets are made using a substantial amount of flowers. They are time-consuming, and can therefore often be very expensive to make. The flowers can be made into a full or half circlet, and both are suitable for brides or bridesmaids. Single-strand circlets such as this are used mainly for small flower girls, as they are light and delicate in design and therefore ideal for younger children.

Materials used:
• florists' tape • 90mm stub wires • sedum • spray roses • small ivy leaves • silver stub wires

how to...

CREATE A CIRCLET HEADDRESS

tip

It is useful to measure the bridesmaid's head with a ribbon, piece of string or tape to establish the amount of material required for the design. Once the tape has been measured against the head, it is then necessary to calculate the amount of wire required for the design. The tape should be laid out flat and wires held up against it until the right length is achieved. In this case, the stub wires used have had to double over to achieve the correct length, which is useful as it lends more support at the front of the head where heavier flowers may be placed. The wires should then be taped together.

① Tape a number of small materials ready to use on the circlet wires. The best way to ensure that enough materials have been prepared is to line them up against the prepared wire and form a pattern.

2

② The wire should be slightly longer than the tape length, so that the ends can be turned backwards to make a hook for securing onto the head. Using a small ivy leaf, place it onto the end of the main wire and cover the hook. Place a small rose bud over the ivy leaf and secure with tape.

3

③ Continue adding all the materials in the same way, winding them on to the wire in a repetitive pattern, alternating textures and colours along the way. The centre area may hold larger flowers to emphasize the front and be more open and focal, or you may wish to continue with the same size flower heads all the way around.

4

④ Using the smallest buds and leaves, as at the start, the end should show that the circle is continuous in materials and it should all flow in a circular fashion. At this point you may wish to secure a small, thin ribbon to trail down the back of the bridesmaid's head. Tuck any wires in neatly once you have joined the circlet.

▷

alternative design

Accessories such as pearls and beads could be incorporated into the design and, additionally, sprayed foliage and flowers such as berries sprayed gold or silver.

Silk flowers are a popular choice, as the head is hot and real flowers can wilt. Silk flowers are very realistic these days and can be best for small, fidgety bridesmaids!

The silk flowers shown here illustrate that small buds are best for small bridesmaids, and that greenery is just as important in these designs as any other.

tips

- Always agree the flowers in the headdress in advance, and make sure that they complement the dress and the person wearing it. The flowers used should always be from the main bouquets, so that they blend well and the theme continues.

- Use light flowers so that the arrangement is not too bulky for a small bridesmaid.

- If making this for a bride, use larger flowers that are more suitable for an adult head.

- Arrange the flowers closer together for a more solid look.

- Be careful not to use anything spiky that would cause any discomfort.

- Use little and few flowers for small bridesmaids, as this emphasizes their fragility and the delicate arrangement is more suitable for their small heads.

comb headdress

This elaborate tiara-shaped headdress on a comb has been made using the same colour scheme and materials as the bridal bouquet to give a perfectly co-ordinated ensemble. A fresh flower design worn in the hair is a unique and pretty alternative to other bridal hair accessories, particularly when a more natural style is being favoured.

Materials used:
• wide comb • floral tape • silver rose wires • blossom • tuberose • spray roses • ivy leaves

how to...

CREATE A COMB HEADDRESS

① Mount individual florets onto silver rose wires and cover with floral tape. Buds can be wired in pairs to add interest to the design and minimize weight.

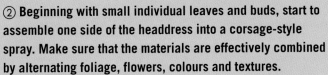

② Beginning with small individual leaves and buds, start to assemble one side of the headdress into a corsage-style spray. Make sure that the materials are effectively combined by alternating foliage, flowers, colours and textures.

③ As the focal area is reached, measure the design against the comb to ensure that it will fit appropriately on one side.

④ Assemble the second spray in exactly the same way, ensuring that it matches the first in shape and size so that, when placed together, they combine to achieve a pleasing tiara-shaped design.

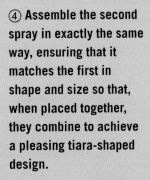

⑤ **Using silver binding wire, attach both sprays snugly together so that the focal flowers and foliage merge into a well-formed centrepiece within the design.**

⑥ **Securely attach the sprays by carefully passing the silver reel wire between the flowers and tightly onto the comb. As some movement of materials is unavoidable during this procedure, reposition any flowers and leaves until the design looks well balanced, symmetrical and curves slightly at either end for fitting on the bride's head.**

tip

A veil can be positioned separately behind the headdress and removed later for the reception, leaving the bride with a hair decoration which is light and easy to wear all evening.

glued comb headdress

A glued comb is suitable either for the bride or for adult bridesmaids. Using glue is an effective and efficient way of fixing materials together and will save precious time. However, bear in mind that the materials are rigid and look static. There is no movement to the design and no flexibility for repositioning materials – once the material has set, it is permanent, so practice before making the final design.

Materials used:
• florists' tape • cold glue or hot glue gun • combs • stub wires • reel wire • ivy leaves • mini gerbera • salal leaves • Singapore orchids

how to...

CREATE A GLUED COMB HEADDRESS

HEALTH AND SAFETY

When using a hot glue gun, make sure that it is switched on in advance to heat up the glue ready for use. Place the gun on to paper so that any drips are caught on the paper and not the table. Have extra glue sticks ready for use, as you always use more than you think you will. When ready, place the end of the flower materials under the dripping glue and stick to the back of the comb. Press down with a florists' knife or the point of the scissors – NEVER use your fingers, as the glue is extremely hot and will burn your fingertips.

① Ensure that all your materials have been prepared ready for use. Small, lightweight flowers are required, while accessories such as feathers, beads and decorative wire may also be added. Wire and tape the leaves, roses and any accessories that you may wish to add. Cut all the flower stems off at the back so that the flower lies as flat as possible on the comb. Using cold glue, or hot glue as illustrated, place the flowers into position, glue and press down firmly on to the comb. Mist the flowers with water and place in a container until ready for use.

tips

- Make sure that you use the appropriate size comb to hold the flowers.

- Experiment with different flowers and create designs that are both practical and striking to look at.

- Cold glue can be better to use – it is less fiddly than hot glue.

- Some flower or plant material may singe or burn if the glue is too hot. Always test your materials first.

- Discuss with the customer what flowers will work with their hair type. Thick, curly hair will require a larger comb, whereas light, fly-away hair will need a small, delicate comb.

- If the hair is too thin it will not hold the comb. A circlet of flowers or individual wired flowers might be more appropriate.

bridesmaid hoop

The children's game of hoop and stick was a popular pastime in the streets of Victorian England, and this sweet design, suitable for a little girl, is reminiscent of it. It is easy to carry, can be decorated simply or extravagantly to suit the style and theme of the wedding and, if made with preserved or fabric materials, will be a lovely keepsake to hang as a door-wreath afterwards.

Materials used:
• plastic-covered hoop • tissue paper • sticky tape • satin ribbon • floral tape • pearl-headed pins • silver rose wires
• selection of fabric flowers

how to...

CREATE A BRIDESMAID HOOP

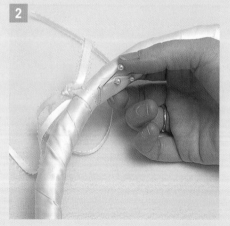

① Cover the hoop with a layer of tissue paper secured with sticky tape, and wrap with satin ribbon, achieving a 'padded' effect which will be comfortable to hold.

② Use pearl-headed pins to neaten ribbon ends, taking care to ensure that they are well secured into the padding to avoid pin pricks to small fingers! Add decorative ribbon bows and trails to the top of the design.

③ Make small sprays of fabric flowers, wiring with silver rose wires if necessary and assembling using floral tape. Leave a wired stem of approximately 10 cm (4 in) for wrapping around the hoop, and cover with ribbon to neaten.

④ **Attach the flower sprays by curling the wire ends around the hoop at equal intervals and cover with small ribbon bows.**

tips

- You can make your own hoop by using thin bundles of 90mm stub wires joined together to the required size and bent into shape. This is useful for making smaller designs for very young children, but not advisable for larger ones as they will be unable to hold their shape when decorated.

- Fresh flowers can be used in a similar way, either in sprays or as a continual layer around the outer edge.

05 funeral designs

funeral flowers

Flowers have been used in funerals for hundreds of years, as they symbolize many things. They play an important role in celebrating the life of the deceased, and they are also used as a mark of respect. Death is very difficult for most people to deal with, and florists must always be aware of the complex emotions that people feel when organizing tributes. With their knowledge and experience, a good florist should be able to make the process less painful for the bereaved.

It is important to select the colours carefully. Pinks, for example, may not be suitable for a deceased male – you may prefer to choose more neutral colours. It is just as important to get this right as it would be for wedding flowers, and even more important than usual to deal with the customer respectfully.

There are many different tributes available these days, everything from rugby balls, guitars, dogs and cricket bats, to cars, wheelbarrows and butterflies. All of these are usually in stock at wholesalers. Years ago people would construct shapes from straw or moss, but nowadays foam shapes are readily available, or designer foam boards can be cut and shaped into the desired forms.

△ Flowers are an age-old means of celebrating the life of a loved one.

Tributes are displayed differently around the world. In Europe we tend to lie tributes on the floor and everything is viewed from above, whereas in the US, for example, they are place on to an upright structured frame and viewed head-on. The tributes illustrated in this section can be used across the world, and viewed from any angle.

△ Foam bases are available in any number of different shapes.

tied sheaf

This tied bouquet is one that can be placed on or beside a coffin. They are more commonly used for cremations, as the flowers are less formal than those often used for a formal burial service. These flowers can be wrapped in cellophane if wished, or left open, as shown here.

Materials used:
• reel wire • foliage • chrysanthemums • hypericum berries • roses • ornamental cabbages • dracaena leaves
• ribbon • twine

how to...

CREATE A TIED SHEAF

When choosing flowers, be careful of thick stems, as this will make the arrangement heavy, and beware of open flowers full of pollen. We would advise that, whatever the occasion, the pollen be removed to prevent damage to clothing or furniture. Once the flowers have been conditioned, place them in separate piles ready for assembling. To begin with, only your scissors and twine are required. You may wish to use reel wire instead, if you prefer. If using particularly delicate stems, the wire may cut into them and therefore twine would be better.

① Assemble the tools and materials that are required for this arrangement. If gift-wrapping these flowers, this is the best time to prepare it, as the surfaces are clean and the wrap will then be immediately ready for the bouquet.

② The technique used for this tied bouquet is similar to plaiting. The wire or twine is secured to one stem of foliage and loose ends are tucked away for safety.

▷

③ Place the first stem vertically, with the second stem laid over it at an angle pointing to the left. The third stem is opposite the second – place it directly over the second stem, at an angle and pointing right. Once the stems are in place, carry the wire around all three stems and bring back to the front to secure the next materials.

④ Add additional foliage as shown to bring more texture and depth to the design, and to act as a backdrop for the flowers. Wind the wire around the material to secure their placements.

⑤ Place more foliage to fill in and create a basic shape, as the bottom points are the edge of your arrangement. Arrange and secure in the same way as before.

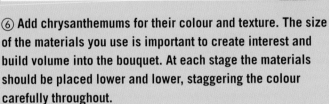

⑥ Add chrysanthemums for their colour and texture. The size of the materials you use is important to create interest and build volume into the bouquet. At each stage the materials should be placed lower and lower, staggering the colour carefully throughout.

⑦ The roses and ornamental cabbages are the most bold in size and colour and therefore are considered the focal flowers. Place these materials strategically through the design, allowing other materials to be threaded through as well. The shape is now becoming much narrower and the materials are being placed at angles towards the edges

⑧ Continue to add more materials, alternating the flower choice and staggering the colours. Bring the materials inwards towards the tie/binding point. The materials may require firm handling at this point to ensure that they do not twist around or fall out of place. At this stage, it may be easier to secure one stem and bind one at a time.

⑨ **Place your focal flowers all the way to the base. The materials that are at the top of the bouquet and at the edge should also be seen at the base. This ensures that the materials 'flow' through your design, and that colour and texture are placed evenly, making the design balance.**

⑩ **Place ornamental leaves at the base to bring the bouquet to a neat finish. Add a bow to complete the bouquet – it should be of a substantial size to balance the colour and length of the bouquet. Spray with water and place flat in a cool area until required.**

ALTERNATIVE MATERIALS

Any flowers can be used for this design, but the colours should suit the occasion and the person that they are intended for. This design is normally used for a funeral, but it could be jazzed up and gift wrapped in cellophane and ribbons and given as a presentation bouquet.

tips

• Using a mixture of large and small flowers is best.

• Open flowers are best, as they use up a lot of space and add instant colour.

• Choose the bow carefully – it is part of the design and should enhance the bouquet, not detract from it.

single-ended spray

The single-ended spray design is teardrop in shape and dense in style, often using lots of foliage. This is normally used for a formal funeral such as a burial, and can be placed on top of a coffin as the main tribute.

Materials used:
- foam • dish • pot tape • leather leaf • spray carnations • carnation blooms • snapdragons (antirrhinums)
- phlox • golden rod (solidaster)

how to...

CREATE A SINGLE-ENDED SPRAY

① Assemble all your materials and condition all flowers and foliage. Soak your foam thoroughly before placing it in the pot and binding securely with pot tape.

② Place a long-stemmed piece of leather leaf foliage at one end for the longest point, with two shorter lengths at the opposite end. Place the leather leaf at the sides, making sure that the design is not too wide. Fill between each point, i.e. from the longest tip to the width piece, and from the width piece to the end pieces. Do this all the way around until you have built your teardrop shape.

③ Place a piece of foliage on the top at an angle, so that the stems are not at sharp angles and not vertical. If this tribute is to be placed on the coffin it must not be too high, as it will not sit comfortably or safely in the hearse. Continue to fill the arrangement with the leather leaf foliage until it is a mass of leaves and no foam can be seen.

④ Using white carnations, place them in the same manner as the foliage until you have your shape. These placements are the 'points' and build shape whilst adding colour.

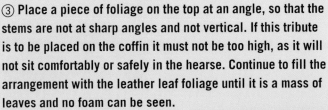

⑤ Always working in odd numbers, place the focal flowers (yellow carnations and snapdragons) into the arrangement. The snapdragons have been used here for their colour, and their long pointy shape makes them perfect to place at the tail end. Place three carnations around a central focal flower in the midpoint of the arrangement, and add two further down towards the end of the arrangement. A final flower should be placed in the tail to bring the colour through and extend the shape. Place the remaining two stems of snapdragon at the tail end. If snapdragons are not available, two more carnations could be used at the tail instead.

▷

⑥ White phlox is a cluster of tiny buds and adds a delicate touch to the design. Use it as filler and place randomly around the other materials, adding light amongst the dark green foliage.

⑦ Finally, add golden rod for texture. The points also accentuate the direction of the shape and complement the other flower materials.

ALTERNATIVE MATERIALS

Use gladioli, iris and delphinium for points; cala lilies, roses and gerberas for focal points; bupleurum, gypsophila and aster for fillers.

tips

- Remember to use pointy materials at the ends to achieve the correct shape and definition.

- Seasonal colours are usually cheaper as they are more plentiful.

- Place the design on the floor whilst arranging to check that the shape is correct and the materials have been evenly distributed.

based heart with spray

What more poignant expression of love can there be than this symbolic tribute from a loved one to their departed? This design with a cushioned base effect and asymmetrical spray containing choice and meaningful flowers is a more expensive option than the other, more informal tributes, and one which requires time and skill to achieve a balanced, harmonious finish.

Materials used:
• floral foam heart base • 90mm stub wires • floral foam block • laurel leaves • hydrangea • echinops globe thistles • viburnum • roses

how to...

CREATE A FOAM-BASED HEART

① Cut a shaped 'bump' from a foam block and attach to the soaked foam heart, using pins made from stub wires passed through into the base until secure. Chamfer the outer edge of the foam with a knife, to make for easier shaping with the basing material.

② Make an edging of single laurel leaves by pinning with stub wires at a slanted angle. They should slightly overlap each other all around the base of the frame.

③ The completed edge should be even and well-spaced, so that the lower rim of the frame is covered sufficiently and no negative space is visible underneath. This is an important aspect to consider with funeral tributes, as they are often placed on the top of the coffin, and therefore the base of the tribute will also be visible.

④ Insert sprigs of hydrangea evenly across the base, making sure that they are bevelled slightly over the rim to produce a softly defined outline. Single echinops globes should be intermingled randomly amongst the hydrangea to add an alternative textural element.

⑤ When the basing is complete, the heart should have a 'padded' appearance with the foam bump clearly visible.

⑥ **Using viburnum leaves and berries, create a diagonal outline of foliage across the top right-hand lobe before your spray of choice, focal flowers is added. This should be kept in scale with the dimensions of the design, the completed spray taking up no more than a third of the finished piece.**

⑦ **Place open roses through the foliage to give a splash of colour and form a focal area on the tribute. A hand-written card can also be placed here with a wire attached at the back, expressing the sender's sentiments in both words and flowers.**

tips

- Pleated ribbon, large single ivy leaves or small foliage sprays can also be used as an edging.

- For a smoother, more traditional basing material, use double chrysanthemum florets butted closely and evenly together.

- Variations of this design can be used as a gift or display item for Valentine's Day or at a wedding venue.

cluster wreath

These tributes are extremely popular as they are so versatile. There are many ways in which you can decorate a wreath, and they can be used both as funeral tributes and for many other occasions. Cluster wreaths can be decorated with foliage and have candles placed in them for advent, or they can have foliage and flowers placed in them and a bowl of water with floating flowers and candles in the centre for a table design. Your imagination can run wild with ideas for any event.

Materials used:
- wreath ring • pot tape • blocks of floral foam • choisya foliage • euonymus and pittosporum foliage
- shamrock chrysanthemum • miniature protea • gerbera • crocosmia • veronica • agapanthus

how to...

CREATE A CLUSTER WREATH

This tribute is shown as a funeral design in two ways, showing how small clusters can adorn the wreath both horizontally (as shown in the step-by-step technique) and vertically (shown in the alternative design).

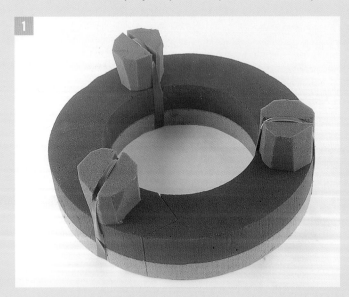

① Arrange your materials and prepare your flowers carefully. Add small 'bumps' of foam to the main wreath frame and secure with pot tape. If your wreath is bigger than the one shown here, it may be necessary to have more bumps, but always have them in odd numbers. Soak the foam frame.

② Cut small lengths of choisya foliage and place into the segment of foam between two bumps.

③ Continue in the same way, using different foliage for each section (we have used euonymus and pittosporum). This adds definition to the wreath and helps to enhance the design.

④ Each bump should have a different colour scheme, and each colour should be in harmony with the others. This design shows bold, striking colours, balanced against each other in terms of colour and texture. The first bump uses shamrock crysanthemum and miniature protea; the second gerbera and crocosmia. The shapes of the miniature arrangements are oval and placements are similar.

⑤ Place veronica and agapanthus on the third bump. Continue adding colour to the wreath and make sure that all three bumps are equal in size, colour and texture. Ensure that there are no gaps in the foliage and that the materials are safe and secure. Spray the arrangement with water.

alternative design

The materials used in this alternative design show that just one flower material can be as effective. The flowers are arranged as one large head on its own, two smaller and three even smaller heads. The stems of the sunflowers are thick, so careful application of these is required. Twigs, moss and pine cones were used to enhance the colour and texture of this design.

tips

- Use a deliberate colour scheme, e.g. analogous (see pages 23–24 for more on colour schemes).

- Ensure that all your materials are fresh, otherwise they will be difficult to work with and will spoil the outcome.

- This design can be used for a display and not a funeral piece, so choose accessories to brighten the design and add humour if necessary.

open cross

The cross is not just a Christian symbol, but is used by many religions and is hugely representative at festivals and special occasions. This design is used in floristry as a formal tribute, normally for a burial, and would be placed by the grave or on top of the coffin. The style used is loose and the flowers are scattered around the arrangement, making for a very free and flowing design.

Materials used:
• cross foam • assorted foliage and berries • spray carnations • lisianthus • chrysanthemums • bear grass

how to...

CREATE AN OPEN CROSS

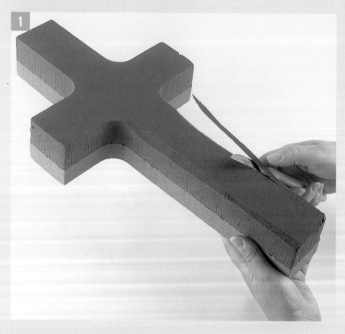

① Bevel the edges of the foam, rounding off the edges in order to help the application of materials. The rounded edges will also seem easier on the eye than straight edges.

② Cut your foliage into small pieces and place it into the foam at different angles. By placing them at angles you are creating movement and stimulating the eye. The frame should be covered entirely.

③ Place yellow spray carnations at the base and top of your design to add colour and brighten up the dark greenery. These 'points' also build shape and add texture.

④ The purple lisianthus are your 'focal' flowers and are in contrast to the bright yellow. These are delicate and soft against the rugged greenery and berries. The line of focal flowers allows the eye to travel up and down the frame.

⑤ Yellow chrysanthemums are a secondary focal point, and complement the dark purple. Place these up and down, in and around the purple.

⑥ Lime green chrysanthemums are your 'fillers' and must be used to enhance the other colours used, to fill any gaps in your foliage and to add texture. These flowers should not dominate but be used in support. The cross frame is now stiff and full of flowers, all of which should have been placed evenly at the same level. Loops of bear grass add height and movement to the design, without detracting from the main arrangement.

ALTERNATIVE MATERIALS

Any flowers can be used for this design, as long as you have 'fillers', 'focals' and 'points'. Soft colours are generally advised for ladies, and more neutral colours for men.

Some alternative materials that work well include:

- Fillers – gypsophila, wax flowers, berries
- Focals – roses, gerberas, lilies
- Points – liatris, iris, spray roses

tips

- Use more delicate flowers if the frame is small, otherwise the foam will crumble.
- Use bright colours – make a statement.
- This is a good way to use up small bits and pieces of foliage from other designs or from the garden.
- Larger cross frames will require a lot more flowers, so calculate the materials required carefully. This frame is 62 cm (2 ft) long.

06 | venue decoration

venue flowers

Venue decorations are particular to the occasion, the customer, the space available and the budget. In this section we will show you a few examples of both hanging and entrance designs. The materials used can be changed to suit your needs and according to seasonal availability.

The designs must never be fixed without the permission of the premises' manager or proprietor, and health and safety must always be considered when placing designs around entrances or hanging at a height. Mechanics should never be seen, so if you must make the hanging secure, use decorative materials to assist you and camouflage your workings.

Measurements must be carefully calculated and costings made simple so that adjustments can be made easily. For example, when calculating a 20 m (66 ft) garland, it is best to calculate the flowers and materials needed per metre, and then this calculation can be added to or taken away from as necessary, should the customer then require it to be longer or shorter than planned.

▷ *Hanging designs are a great addition to a florist's portfolio.*

△ *Always make sure that your mechanics and fastenings are well hidden.*

hanging swag

When a smaller hanging spray would suit the situation better than a full-scale garland, a swag made from fresh or dried materials, or a mixture of both, can be a very striking, seasonal accent on a wall, table, chair-back or mantelpiece. This can be constructed by wiring materials on to a length of rope, although the method shown here, using a mossed base, will ensure that fresh materials are able to absorb moisture and so will last much longer.

Materials used:
- sphagnum moss • twine • wreath wrap • 90mm stub wires • mixed garden foliage and berries • roses • raffia
- pine cones • cinnamon sticks • dried orange slices • poppy seed heads

how to...

CREATE A HANGING SWAG

① Construct a sausage-shaped base using handfuls of fresh sphagnum moss, which has first been teased out and any twigs or leaves removed. The base is assembled using twine, tugging tightly to secure until the required length is achieved.

② On the reverse flat side, attach plastic wreath wrap with pins made from stub wire. This will ensure a smooth, dry backing which will protect the surface that the swag will be attached to from being damaged by moisture from the moss.

③ Attach wire loops for hanging the design to each end of the swag base, with a raffia bow placed over them to conceal the wires.

④ It is essential to make sure that these loops are secured by returning the wires back into the mossed base for a firm anchorage.

⑤ You will need to pre-wire decorative dried and fresh items for attaching in single units and sprays. Pine cones are mounted by sliding long-length stub wires between the layers of seed scales, and twisting around the cone's centre.

⑥ Twist the wire into a double leg mount, which will provide good support and firm anchorage when positioned in the base. Any protruding wires should be returned safely back into the moss. All materials can be wired using this method, including bundles of cinnamon sticks tied with raffia and clusters of dried fruits or nuts, as well as natural foliage sprays and individual flower heads.

⑦ Add a large seed head and pine cone at either end to define the curved points of the swag, and to further conceal the wire loops.

▷

⑧ **Beginning at each end and working towards the centre, position material evenly at the sides and down the middle of the base, ensuring that there are no gaps by slightly overlapping each piece as you go.**

⑨ **Place a large raffia bow at the centre to create a focal point, and add fresh rose heads along the whole length for a splash of vibrant colour.**

⑨ **Continue to position the decorative fresh and dried material amongst the foliage and berries until a balanced and harmonious design is created.**

alternative design

By using fresh, seasonal flowers and foliages, this design would be suitable for a wedding decoration, perhaps on the registrar's desk at a civil ceremony or even to adorn the chair-backs of the bride and groom at the wedding breakfast afterwards. Ribbons have been integrated to echo the colour scheme in the other bridal flowers and accessories.

tips

- Fading flowers can be replaced with fresh, so that the swag can continue to be enjoyed for several weeks over the festive season, or after the occasion it was created for.

- This design can also be used as a centrepiece for a rectangular or oval dining table, although care must be taken to ensure that wires are concealed so as to avoid scratching the surface

test-tube garland

Decorative garlands have been popular for adorning homes and venues since classical times. The early Romans decorated their hallways with holly garlands at their winter festivals, not unlike the Christmas versions we use today to decorate our banisters and mantels. This garland, incorporating glass test-tubes of flowers, has been designed to frame the mirror in a bride's bedroom, but the design is endlessly versatile. It can be made to any length or in any style, and is suitable for beautifying any number of places.

Materials used:
• paper-covered reel wire • coloured aluminium wire • glass test-tubes • floral glitter and spray glue • mixed foliage • roses • carnations • sea-holly (eryngium) • gypsophila

how to...

CREATE A TEST-TUBE GARLAND

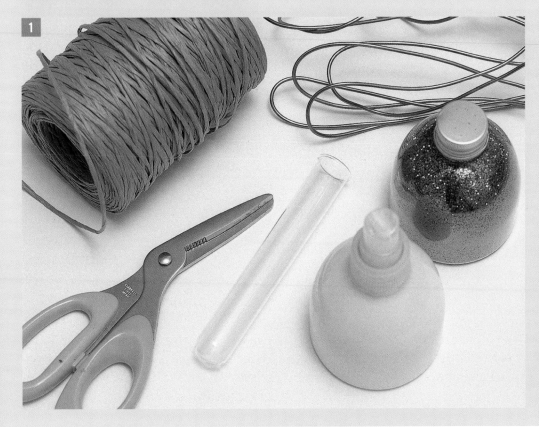

① Gather all your materials together, and ensure that your flowers and foliage are close at hand.

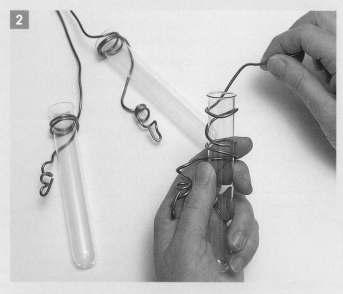

② Prepare the tubes by twisting aluminium wire securely several times around the top of the tube, just below the rim, and allowing excess wire to form a hook for hanging onto the garland.

③ Spray the roses with a fine mist of glue, then shake floral glitter over them to embellish.

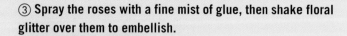

④ Attach paper-covered reel wire to the first stems of foliage, winding it round and fixing securely.

⑤ Add more foliage and wire it in until the required length is achieved. This method produces a very flexible garland which can be hung in swags or wrapped around pillars, arches and banisters.

⑥ Wire individual heads of sea-holly and insert them at intervals along the garland length, twisting the wire legs around foliage stems to secure.

⑦ Use pot tape to mount the garland on to the mirror (or other surface), then attach the test-tubes to the foliage, in between the sea-holly and down the length of the whole garland.

tips

- For a hanging garland, robust flower heads such as chrysanthemums and spray carnations can be wired and attached all along the design in place of the test-tubes.

- Use dried and preserved materials to create an autumnal, harvest or thanksgiving-themed design.

- Accessories can be added for sparkle and glitter in an evening venue, e.g. strands of beads, sequins, baubles and metallic ribbons.

⑧ Fill the test-tubes two thirds full with water and arrange two or three blooms in each one.

topiary tree

As a feature design alone, or in a pair, the topiary tree contributes style and elegance to any venue, whether it be the simplest of marquees or the grandest of castles and stately homes. They can be sited singly in an alcove, against a plain wall, in a pair on either side of a doorway or fireplace, or even at each end of a banqueting table.

Materials used:
- large plastic or ceramic pot • ready-mix cement • broom handle • foam sphere • satin ribbon
- pearl-headed pins • fabric for covering pot • mixed foliage • lilies • roses • phlox

how to...

MAKE A TOPIARY TREE

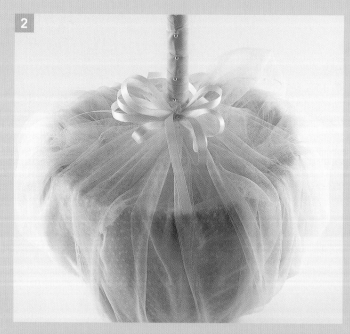

① Fix the broom handle into the base of the pot with cement, stabilizing with tape strips across the top of pot if necessary until set fast. Cover the pole completely with ribbon and secure with tape at the base, embellishing with pearl-headed pins.

② Using a co-ordinating fabric, cover the pot completely, finishing off with satin ribbon bows and trails.

③ Push a pre-soaked foam sphere on to the top of the pole, and cover it with an outline of foliage to establish the required size, shape and form.

④ Begin to build the design up by adding focal flowers around the globe, making sure that materials are distributed evenly throughout.

▷

⑤ To help with filling in and to add textural contrast, satin ribbon bows mounted on to stub wires can be placed deep into the design wherever gaps are evident. Adding ribbon trails to the base of the sphere gives a softer contrast between the globe and the pole.

⑥ Fill in any remaining negative space with foliage until the tree is complete.

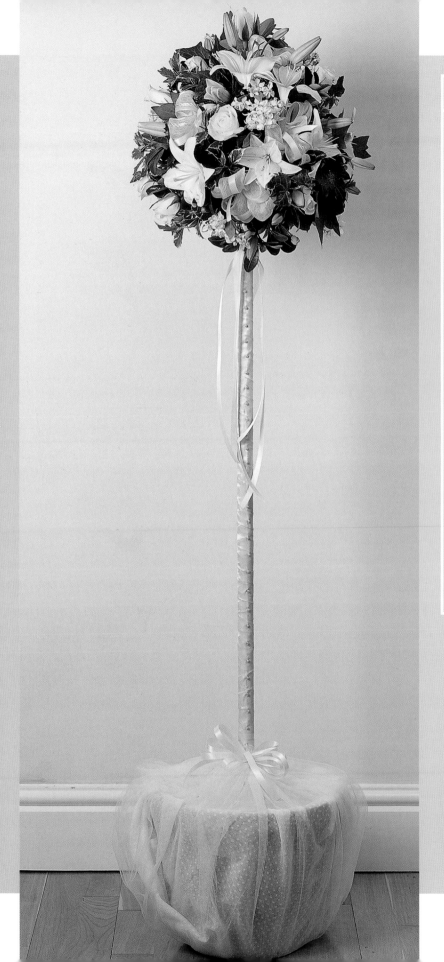

tips

- Trees can also be constructed as 'flat' spheres, which use less material but are best suited when the design will only be viewed face-on, as they do not have the three-dimensional quality of a globe construction.

- This design can be used for any season or occasion where the setting requires height but not the width that a pedestal arrangement would provide.

- Ensure that the base contains enough cement to support the top. If unbalanced, the weight will make the design unstable and it may fall over.

- Try not to wet the sphere of foam too much or use any thick-stemmed and heavy flowers at the top. The weight of either of these can make the ball slide down the pole, ruining your design.

$\triangleright$

alternative design

In this alternative design, a pre-bought artificial garland has been wound around the foam and secured with wire pins. Artificial Christmas roses, berries and nuts are arranged in the centre of the garland sphere and finished with a Christmas ribbon bow. Co-ordinating ribbon and organza fabric adorns the pole and the container.

glossary

accessories Decorative elements.
achromatic colours Neutral colours.
analogous colours Three or four different colours that lie next to each other on the colour wheel.
arrangement Flower materials assembled in a medium or container.

binding point The point at which the binding material holds the units together, either in a wired or hand-tied design.
binding wire Stub or silver wire on a reel.
bloom An open flower.
bud An unopened bloom.

choicest Most expensive or distinctive.
cluster A small arrangement used on funeral tributes. Also called the bump or spray.
commission Special order for an individual client.
complementary colours Opposite colours on the colour wheel.
contract Regular order, usually for a company or venue.

depth Flowers that are used deep inside an arrangement to make it look bigger and more involved.
design Specific shape or style of arrangement.
dominance A characteristic in a design that competes with other materials and seems more bold and therefore 'dominant'.

exotics Flowers from tropical climates.

fillers Less expensive materials used to fill out a design.
floral foam Medium used to support stems in a variety of designs.
flower food In powder or liquid form, containing anti-bacterial agents and minerals.
focal Material that forms the central aspect of a design.
foliage Cut greenery from shrubs or trees.
frame Shaped wire base.

gutta percha Rubber-based tape for binding and concealing stems.

interest Sundry materials used for distinction.

linear Vertical or horizontal lines.
loose Open style incorporating space within the design.

minimalist Modern style making use of few elements.
monochromatic colours Tints, tones and shades, all of one colour.

nosegay Traditional scented posy.

polychromatic colours Many different colours assembled together.
pot tape Strong waterproof tape for securing foam, etc. into containers.
proportion The dimensions of the materials within a design and also the scale of the design surroundings.

radiate Stems coming from a central point.
recession Elements used to give visual depth, bringing the focus from the centre points to the edge by using different colours and sizes.
rhythm The movement and interest created by materials within a design.
rustic Natural, country-style materials.

secondaries Slightly less expensive materials than focals.
shower Bridal bouquet with a trail.
silver wires Finer gauge wires primarily used for wedding work.
space A key feature of floristry, referring to the space around each flower within the design and the space around the outside of it.
sphagnum moss Plant material used as a medium for wired designs.
stamen Male organ of a flower containing pollen.
stub wires Wires used to support and anchor stems.

test tubes Glass vials incorporated into designs as accessories.
texture Visual or actual substance of materials.
toolbox Portable container of basic equipment.
traditional Classic style or technique.

unit Several pieces of wired flower material bound together.

variety Mixture or assortment of materials, styles or shapes.

wreath Circular design signifying eternal life.

index

acknowledgements

All photography is by Shona Wood.

Authors' acknowledgements

Jacqueline Goss
With love and thanks to Chris for his constant
encouragement and continuing support.
And for Jodie and Lauren, whom I love up to the
moon and back!

Jane Wighton
For my daughter Hannah – a florist from birth!
Fondest memories of Mum – still missed.
And with love to my dear Terry, Ben, Abi and Stuart
"...my cup runneth over" (Psalm 23).

New Holland Publishers would like to thank Hannah Eley,
Abigail Wighton, Jodie Goss and Lauren Goss for modelling,
Ridley Hall Evangelical Church for use of their facilities and
location for photography, and Penny Brown for the index.